Evil in America

Evil in America

Ben Shapiro

Creators Publishing
Hermosa Beach, CA

Evil in America
Copyright © 2017
All rights reserved. No part of this book may be reproduced or transmitted in any form or by any means, electronic or mechanical, including photocopying, recording or by any information storage and retrieval system, without permission in writing from the author.

Cover art by Peter Kaminski

CREATORS PUBLISHING
737 3rd St
Hermosa Beach, CA 90254
310-337-7003

This is a work of fiction. Names, characters, businesses, places, events and incidents are either the products of the author's imagination or used in a fictitious manner. Any resemblance to actual persons, living or dead, or actual events is purely coincidental.

Library of Congress Control Number: 2017939426
ISBN (print): 978-1-945630-57-6
ISBN (ebook): 978-1-945630-56-9

First Edition
Printed in the United States of America
10 9 8 7 6 5 4 3 2 1

Contents

~~~

A Note From the Publisher

Since 1987, Creators has syndicated many of your favorite columns to newspapers. In this digital age, we are bringing collections of those columns to your fingertips. This will allow you to read and reread your favorite columnists, with your own personal digital archive of their work.

Creators Publishing

Self-Love vs. Self-Betterment

January 7, 2015

On Dec. 31, as 2014 began to fade into the past, New York Times columnist Charles Blow tweeted out some deep thoughts from his new book, "Fire In My Bones." "Daring to step into oneself is the bravest, strangest, most natural, most terrifying thing a person can do," Blow wrote regarding his acknowledgement of his own bisexuality, "because when you cease to wrap yourself in artifice you are naked, and when you are naked you are vulnerable. But vulnerability is the leading edge of truth. Being willing to sacrifice a false life is the only way to live a true one." He then added, "It takes more courage to be yourself than it does to do almost anything else. Being yourself, your whole self, without compromise or apology, is a revolutionary act!"

This line of thought doesn't originate with Blow, of course. Jean-Jacques Rousseau spoke similarly; his concept of amour de soi suggested that self-love—that is, love for oneself without reference to outside sources—was the highest form of happiness, and that only amour de soi could drive good action.

This is nonsense; it always was nonsense; it always will be nonsense. No doubt self-destructive tendencies can harm both the individual and society more broadly. But conversely, self-love as the highest form of bravery undermines the notion of objective good and self-sacrifice in pursuit of that objective good. If being yourself is the highest aspiration for mankind, then anyone who stands between you and your own self-regard becomes an enemy. Society must be shifted on its ear to accommodate your perception of yourself.

And so we enter the backwards world in which individual self-perception trumps objective reality. To pick a fringe example, if a fully biological man perceives himself to be a woman, all of society must hereby acknowledge him as a woman, a nonsensical proposition. Logically speaking, a man cannot declare himself a woman without a point of internal reference; it makes no more sense to do this than to declare oneself a purple-headed space alien, given that human beings have no idea what it like to be a purple-headed space alien without being one. All of society is expected to flout reality in order to preserve the self-love of the mentally ill.

More problematic, all of society is expected to adjust to the expected returns self-love brings. If we all believe ourselves geniuses, we expect to be compensated as such. If society fails to comprehend our genius, that is society's fault. To borrow from Jim Croce, we all end up with the steadily depressing, low down, mind messing, working at the car wash blues. That is, until we call on government to recognize that we are each an undiscovered Howard Hughes.

Being comfortable with oneself is not bravery. If it means ignoring the call of a higher purpose, it is cowardice. There are millions of American students who are comfortable with their level of educational and intellectual achievement. That's why they're falling behind their compatriots in other industrialized countries. There are millions of Americans perfectly comfortable with abandoning their children, or murdering their unborn children. That does not make their action right, or public policy designed to stop such action wrong.

Self-betterment used to be the motto of Western civilization. That's because Western civilization used to be based on the premise that man is more than animal. But in freeing man from the shackles of humanity, we have achieved just what Rousseau sought. And so we may yet live like animals again, perhaps happy in the bravery of our amour de soi, but somewhat less happy in the failure of humanity's truly noble aspirations.

Charlie Hebdo Lost

January 14, 2015

The West has the capacity to win a war on radical Islam. But it won't.

It won't because the West is too busy soul-searching to defend its core values. Western leaders mouth slogans about #JeSuisCharlie in the aftermath of the murder of 12 at the Charlie Hebdo headquarters, but they don't mean it; they suggest that the world stands united against radical Islamic terror even as they ignore the bullet-ridden bodies of four at a kosher supermarket in Paris.

The proof: Look at the list of those who attended Sunday's unity march in Paris.

The usual suspects showed up, except for President Obama, who was presumably too busy golfing or watching football. So, too, did several leaders explicitly connected with radical Islam and terrorism.

Palestinian Authority President Mahmoud Abbas, showed up to tell the French people, "Human life is sacred and God has created us all." But that's not what he tells his constituents. Last week, Al-Asima, a publication distributed by the Palestinian Authority, celebrated the murderers of five people at a synagogue in Jerusalem. Abbas routinely meets with terrorists who are released from prison after murdering Jews. As Hamas rained rockets down on Israel, Abbas justified it, telling the United Nations that Palestinians had the "legitimate right to resist this colonial, racist Israeli occupation."

But those are just dead Jews, so welcome to France!

Then there's Turkish Prime Minister Ahmet Davutoglu, who represents a regime that has provided material support to Hamas, including the infamous terror flotilla. Turkey's leader, Recep Tayyip Erdogan, says that the very term "moderate Islam" is "very ugly, it is offensive and an insult to our religion. There is no moderate or immoderate Islam. Islam is Islam and that's it." Turkey's refusal to fight ISIS has led to the rise of that terror group as well.

Sheikh Abdullah bin Zayed al-Nahyan of the United Arab Emirates came to Paris as well. Harvard University rejected Al-Nahyan's $2.5 million donation in 2004 after it emerged that al-Nahyan was associated with a think tank that pushed anti-American and anti-Semitic diatribes.

All three of these regimes, by the way, believe that blasphemy against Mohammed should be criminalized. Allowing them to march in honor of Charlie Hebdo demonstrates the moral idiocy of the West.

But the media hailed the march, nonetheless, as a ground shift in world relations. After all, so many leaders had linked arms in a pro forma tribute to free speech, it just had to mean something.

Except that it doesn't. It doesn't mean a damn thing. It means only that the West is too stupid or empty-hearted to stand up for its principles; we will welcome anyone to our club, even those who want to join the club only to burn it down.

That, in a nutshell, is the problem with the West's policy with regard to radical Islam. When I asked Islamic imam Anjem Choudary—a man who has essentially defended the Charlie Hebdo terrorists—why the West should allow him to live in Britain while attempting to tear down all of its values, he simply stated that he was born in England. He then added, "You can change your laws," and threatened that if no laws were changed to ban material like that of Charlie Hebdo, there would certainly be a "bloodbath."

And the West agrees. Anyone can join our free speech marches, our freedom of religion candlelight vigils—even people who would blow up both of them at the first available opportunity.

The Last Taboo

January 21, 2015

What happens when we run out of taboos?

The question arises thanks to a column in Salon.com from one Jenny Kutner, an assistant editor "focusing on sex, gender and feminism." This particular column focuses on an 18-year-old woman who is currently dating. That wouldn't be odd, except that she is dating her biological father. Apparently, this woman's father left her family when she was 4; when he came back into her life, she was 16. "It was so weird and confusing," she said. "I was seeing my dad for the first time in forever but it was also like, He's so good looking!"

Days later, they had sex. "We discussed whether it was wrong and then we kissed," the woman said. "And then we made out, and then we made love for the first time. That was when I lost my virginity."

Kutner, naturally, describes the activity as merely a manifestation of Genetic Sexual Attraction. She adds, "As sensational as the whole interview might seem (and, admittedly, as it is), it actually forces one to do some rigorous double-checking of one's own beliefs."

Why, exactly, would one double check one's own beliefs when faced with the reality of incest? Any normal society would immediately question the evil father, who abandoned his child, only to come back into her life and take advantage of her sexually. Any normal society would recognize the evil of a father having sex with his genetic offspring. Any normal society would place the onus on those arguing for incest to explain why society is bettered by normalization of incest, rather than placing the onus on the traditionally moral to explain why incest should remain taboo.

But we are not a normal society any longer. We are a society of love.

Love, we now believe, conquers all—including basic standards of morality. As Attorney General Eric Holder said this week in explaining why the Supreme Court should strike down traditional marriage laws, "It is time for our nation to take another critical step forward to ensure the fundamental equality of all Americans—no matter who they are, where they come from, or whom they love." Who are we to judge those who love one another? So long as they can always abort their damaged offspring; so long as the couple believes itself to be operating under standards of consent; so long as an incestuous relationship doesn't affect you directly, who are you to judge?

The normalization of incest does not spring from the normalization of homosexuality, of course. Both the normalization of incest and the normalization of homosexuality spring from the destruction of objective standards of morality in favor of validation of subjective feelings. Society is bettered by heterosexual marriage because man and woman can exclusively create and best raise children. The same is not true of any other form of relationship. But that doesn't matter, because radical relativism is our new standard.

And so we search for new taboos to break. Undoubtedly, the next standard will be normalization of younger and younger teens having sex with older partners. After that, we will see polygamy.

Eventually, the only true taboo left will be responsibility. But that's a taboo no one will be willing to violate, given the social stigma attached. Better to live free, basking in the glow of transgressive bravery. After all, if you're truly brave, you fight the system. And when there is no system, you fight the meaninglessness. And you lose.

Will Republicans Go the Way of the Whigs?

January 28, 2015

In 1856, the Whig Party ran former president Millard Fillmore for president of the United States. Fillmore had last run in 1852; he'd been denied the nomination as the party fell apart over the issue of slavery. In an attempt to bring the party back together that year, the party nominated General Winfield Scott, who promptly imploded in the general election against Democrat Franklin Pierce. "We are slain!" shouted Representative Lewis D. Campbell of Ohio. "The party is dead, dead, dead!" Free Soiler Charles Sumner wrote, "Now is the time for a new organization. Out of this chaos the party of freedom must arise."

Most of the Whig leaders thought this talk overwrought. They insisted that the party would live on. Senator William Seward of New York said, "No new party will arise, nor will any old one fall." Seward thought that if the party elided the slavery issue, it could hold together. But by the same token, without the slavery issue, there was truly no difference between the two parties. As future president Rutherford B. Hayes wrote, "The real grounds of difference upon important political questions no longer correspond with party lines. The progressive Whig is nearer in sentiment to the radical Democrat than the radical Democrat is to the 'fogy' of his own party; vice versa." The party had become a party of convenience rather than principle.

Between 1852 and 1856, as author William E. Gienapp discusses, the break came: Southern Whigs joined the pro-slavery Democrats, while northern Whigs joined the newly formed anti-slavery Republicans. In 1856, the Whig candidate won just one state, while the Republican candidate, John C. Fremont, carried 11 states. James Buchanan carried 19 states. By 1860, the Whigs no longer existed. Abraham Lincoln won the presidency with less than 40 percent of the vote.

This is what happens to parties that lose their reason for being: They disintegrate. The modern Republican Party may be in serious danger of falling into that trap. That's not because of the Republican constituency, which reflects, as it has since the 1980s, the three-pronged approach of fiscal conservatism, foreign policy hawkishness and social traditionalism. It's because the Republican political class seem to reject those unifying factors as divisive.

How else to explain the GOP House's decision last week, in the aftermath of a massive electoral sweep, to table a piece of legislation banning abortion after the 20th week of pregnancy? This is an issue upon which most Americans are united—the vast majority of Americans find late-term abortion morally abhorrent. And yet Representative Renee Ellmers, R-N.C., removed her name from the bill, stating, "We got into trouble last year" over issues like abortion. If Republicans won't stand together on such a basic moral issue, over what issues *will* they unite?

Certainly not illegal immigration, where Republicans divide from their base, pushing a softer approach to President Obama's executive amnesty. Certainly not foreign policy, where President Obama's devastation of the military has been met with Republican resistance but not Republican intransigence. Certainly not Obamacare, where Speaker of the House Boehner recently provided full funding for the last year.

The Republican higher-ups assure us, as Whig leaders did in 1852, that if Republicans nominate someone with name recognition, an old warhorse perhaps, the party can unify once again. Jeb Bush or Mitt Romney fill in for Winfield Scott. But just as Whigs were only able to win two presidential elections over the course of 23 years, both times with military heroes at the head, Republicans have won just one popular presidential election in the last 27 years, that time with a commander-in-chief incumbent during wartime.

Perhaps the Republican Party isn't dead. But Republican leaders would be wise to take a lesson from the Whigs if they hope to avoid their fate.

Anti-Vaccine Fanatics Kill

February 4, 2015

This week, controversy broke out over whether state governments have the power to require parents to have their children vaccinated. New Jersey Governor Chris Christie, no stranger to compelling his citizens to stay off the roads during blizzards, announced that he had some sympathy for the anti-vaccination position: "I also understand that parents need to have some measure of choice in things as well. So that's the balance the government has to decide." Kentucky Senator Rand Paul doubled down on Christie's remarks, stating, "I have heard of many tragic cases of walking, talking, normal children who wound up with profound mental orders after vaccines. ...The state doesn't own your children."

Christie and Paul aren't the only politicians sympathizing with anti-vaccination fanatics; in 2008, then-Senator Barack Obama repeated widely debunked claims of links between autism and vaccination. Skepticism of vaccination crosses party lines, unfortunately—although the most organized anti-vaccination resistance comes from the New Agey left in places like Santa Monica and Marin County, who worry more about infinitesimal amounts of formaldehyde in vaccines than about death by polio.

Unsurprisingly, older Americans believe that children should be vaccinated against diseases like measles, mumps and whopping cough, by a 73 percent to 21 percent margin. Americans 18-29, by contrast, believe by a 43 percent to 42 percent plurality that government should not mandate such vaccinations.

That's because young people don't remember a time when such diseases claimed lives. They don't remember a time when the vast majority of Americans weren't vaccinated. Older people do. Many of them lost loved ones to polio and measles and mumps and rubella. In 1952, over 3,000 Americans died of polio and well over 21,000 were left with mild or severe paralysis. Thanks to Dr. Jonas Salk's vaccine, there have been zero cases of natural polio in the United States since 1979.

The same is true of measles. According to Dr. Mark Papania of the Centers for Disease Control and Prevention, more than 90 percent of Americans suffered from the measles by age 15 before widespread vaccination beginning in 1962. From 1956 to 1960, he reports, "an average of 542,000 cases were reported annually." That included 450 deaths per year, as well as 150,000 cases of respiratory complications and 4,000 cases of consequent encephalitis per year, many of which resulted in later death. Then mandatory vaccination kicked in. Until a major upswing in 2014, we averaged less than 100 cases of measles per year in the United States since 2000.

The point of mandatory vaccinations is not merely to protect those who are vaccinated. When it comes to measles, mumps and rubella, for example, children cannot be vaccinated until 1 year of age. The only way to prevent them from getting diseases is to ensure that those who surround them do not have those diseases. The same is true for children with diseases like leukemia, as well as pregnant women. Herd immunity is designed to protect third parties.

But Americans have short memories and enormous confidence in junk science. Parents will ignore vaccinations but ensure that their kids are stocked up with the latest homeopathic remedies, Kabbalah bracelets and crystals. St. John's wort, red string and crystals all existed before 1962. They didn't stop the measles. Vaccination did.

That doesn't mean that all vaccinations should be compulsory, of course. There are certain diseases that can only be transmitted by behavior, like HPV. There are others that are too varied for effective herd vaccination, like the flu shot. But when it comes to measles and mumps and rubella and polio, your right to be free of vaccination—and your right to be a dope with the health of your child because you believe Jenny McCarthy's idiocy—ends where my child's right to live begins.

Shut Up, Because the Crusades

February 11, 2015

This week, President Obama spoke at the National Prayer Breakfast, where he proceeded to inform an audience of Christians that they ought not judge radical Muslims currently engaged in beheading journalists, defenestrating gays, crucifying children, and engaging in mass rape of women. Why, pray tell, should Christians remain silent? Because, Obama informed them with Ivy League pride, "Unless we get on our high horse and think that this is unique to some other place, remember that during the Crusades and Inquisition, people committed terrible deeds in the name of Christ. In our home country, slavery and Jim Crow all too often was justified in the name of Christ. So it is not unique to one group or one religion."

At some point in our collective history, our ancestors engaged in tribal warfare and cannibalized their fallen enemies. So shut up about the Nazis, you hypocrites.

Forget Obama's historical ignorance, if you can, for just a moment. Forget that the Crusades, for all their brutality and horror, were a response to Islamic aggression; forget that the Inquisition was an attempt to systematize legal punishment for anti-Christian activity rather than leaving it to the heated mob; forget that all abolitionist leaders were devout Christians; forget that hundreds of thousands of Christians marched to their deaths during the Civil War singing the words "as He died to make men holy, so we die to make men free"; forget that the chief leaders of the civil rights movement were Christian leaders like Reverend Martin Luther King Jr.

Focus instead on the fact that President Obama felt the necessity to defend radical Islam at all. Why defend radical Islam? What is the point?

Obama defends radical Islam because he does not think in terms of ideology, but in terms of power dynamics. If radical Muslims commit terror, it is because they feel helpless and hopeless. If they feel helpless and hopeless, it is because Westerners made them feel that way. If Westerners made them feel that way, it is because Western ideology must be exploitative and evil.

In other words, Obama cites the Crusades as justification for shutting Christians up because the Crusades caused all of this. If Christians had just kept their pieholes shut several thousand years ago, none of this would have happened. Obama's ignorant and bigoted gloss on Christian history isn't a throwaway line: it's the centerpiece of his philosophy. Radical Islam isn't the problem because Christianity is. And we know that Christianity is the problem because radical Islam is violent. In this skewed version of reality, modern Christianity's fantastic record is a direct outgrowth of its disreputable past.

Obama extends this bizarre philosophy to every part of life. Those who murder Jews in Israel aren't motivated by radical Islam: They were exploited by those evil, non-murdering Jews. Those who riot in Ferguson aren't motivated by a corrupt ideology of victimhood: They were exploited long ago by those who cower in their stores, trying to prevent the looting. Those who sire children they abandon, drop out of school and refuse to hold down jobs aren't predictable refuse of a broken philosophy: They are victims of those who get married, stay in school and hold down jobs. Success is the ultimate indicator that your philosophy is evil. Failure is the ultimate indicator that you are a victim, regardless of your ideology.

Obama's philosophy is the philosophy of failure. No wonder radical Islam holds a cherished place in his heart, while Judeo-Christian religion find itself in his doghouse.

Is Israel the Problem, or Are Jews the Problem?

February 18, 2015

In the aftermath of the killing of a man at a Copenhagen synagogue by a member of the Religion of Peace, Israeli Prime Minister Benjamin Netanyahu said, "This wave of attacks is expected to continue. Jews deserve security in every country, but we say to our Jewish brothers and sisters, Israel is your home." Russian emigre Natan Sharansky echoed Netanyahu's call, stating, "There is no future for Jews in western Europe."

In response, European leaders shouted down Netanyahu. "We know there are doubts, questions across the community," said French President Francois Hollande, who was elected with in excess of 93 percent of the Muslim vote. "I will not just let what was said in Israel pass, leading people to believe that Jews no longer have a place in Europe and France, in particular." The same week, Jewish tombstones were spray-painted by the hundreds in eastern France.

But undoubtedly, European anti-Semites will now claim that Netanyahu's comments simply demonstrate *why* Europe must force out its Jews: because Israel is just so awful. That, at least, is what a German court in the city of Wuppertal concluded after convicting two German Palestinians of setting fire to a synagogue. The Wuppertal court stated that the men were simply attempting to bring "attention to the Gaza conflict." In other words, Jews are fair game because of Israel.

But it's precisely the reverse that is true: Israel is fair game because it is Jewish. This is the dirty little secret of anti-Israel policy: It is almost entirely anti-Semitic policy. That is why Muslims attack Jewish synagogues in Paris during the Gaza war: because

Israel is a stand-in for the Jews, not the other way around. Were Israel a Muslim country, the rest of the world would see it as a beacon of light and hope for the future of an entire religion. Because it is Jewish, Muslims target it for destruction, and the rest of the world tut-tuts Israel's nasty habit of attempting to survive. The extra-American world hates Israel because it is Jewish. It does not hate Jews because of Israel. Israel is merely a convenient excuse.

Ironically, radical Muslims, in targeting Jews throughout the world, reinforce the necessity of a state of Israel. Their argument seems to be that Israel is an unnecessary Jewish nationalist cancer; to prove that argument, they suggest killing Jews all over the planet, leaving no place safe for Jews except for Israel.

And so Jews go to Israel by the droves. European governments can rip Netanyahu all they want for his supposedly brusque dismissal of European tolerance, but that supposed tolerance means less and less when Swedish Jews abandon entire cities as the authorities make way for radical Muslims. European governments can condemn the Gaza war, but Jews see that war for what it was: an exercise in Jewish self-preservation, with the Europeans once again attempting to prevent such self-preservation.

Unlike the Europeans, Americans continue to side with Israel because America is founded on Judeo-Christian principles. America embraces Judaism, and so it embraces Israel, not the other way around. The formula is simple: Love Jews; love Israel. Hate Jews; hate Israel. Opposing Israeli action may not be anti-Semitism, but it sure does have a funny habit of backing the agenda of anti-Semites.

Why Rudy and Walker Were Right

February 25, 2015

This week, the media broke news that former New York Mayor Rudy Giuliani said, at an event attended by prospective Republican presidential candidate Wisconsin Governor Scott Walker, that he does not believe President Barack Obama "loves America." This isn't news. Barack Obama doesn't love free enterprise, believes founding philosophy was fatally flawed and sees the American people as rubes with antiquated religious and racist tendencies. Sure, we can all agree that Obama likely loves America's scenery; perhaps he loves America, but doesn't like her very much. But that's not what Giuliani was talking about, and everyone knows it.

But in any case, Giuliani wasn't the media's true target. The true target was Walker.

Using Giuliani's comments as a springboard, media members went hunting for a faux pas from Walker. They asked him whether he thinks Obama loves America; Walker responded, quite rightly, "You should ask the president what he thinks about America. I've never asked him so I don't know." They asked him whether he believed Obama was a Christian; Walker answered, "I don't know. ... You've asked me to make statements about people that I haven't had a conversation with about that."

For the media, this represented a "gotcha" moment. Anyone who doubts President Obama's love of country must be pilloried as cruel and inhumane. Anyone who doubts the religious sincerity of a man who invoked Christianity to support lies about his support for traditional marriage, a man who recently compared Christian history with the acts of ISIS, must be publicly scourged.

Naturally, many Republicans have eagerly jumped on the bandwagon. George F. Will said that all Republicans should say that Obama is a patriot (a strategy that worked brilliantly for John McCain in 2008). Matt Lewis of The Daily Beast wrote that no candidate should question anyone's patriotism or stated faith. The premise seems to be that failing to demonstrate such goodwill touches off media conflagrations that damage conservatives overall. This misses the point.

Democrats have for years been questioning the decency of Republicans as human beings. During the Obamacare rollout, President Obama accused Republicans of wanting to deprive people of healthcare; he openly accused President George W. Bush of being "unpatriotic" for raising the national debt. House Minority Leader Nancy Pelosi said that Republicans are "indifferent" to hungry and poor children. Anyone who opposes any aspect of President Obama's agenda has been deemed a racist.

The point here is not the media's double standard, which is egregious but unchangeable. The point is that this perception of Republicans has pervaded the public arena. Republicans' fundamental burden is not explaining to the American people that Democrats are great people, but wrong on policy. Their great burden is overcoming the generalized perception that they are money-grubbing Snidely Whiplashes bent on strapping widows and orphans to the train tracks.

You cannot overcome that perception by ardently pleading that the very folks who call you racist, sexist, homophobic bigots are well-intentioned but incompetent. If someone calls you a racist, and you respond by stating that they are a reasonable human being with policy differences, you grant their premise: A reasonable person has called you a racist, which means it is reasonable to call you racist. You lose.

And Republicans have been losing, at least in large part, because they grant the fundamental premise of the left: Democrats are well-meaning, even when they are wrong, and Republicans have evil intentions, even when they are right. That is a recipe for disaster in a country where intentions matter more than actions.

The Hillary Cover-Up and the End of Democracy

March 4, 2015

On Monday, The New York Times reported that former Secretary of State Hillary Clinton never—not once—used her official State Department email address for her official communications. Instead, she utilized a private email account, effectively protecting her emails from public scrutiny. The Washington Post then broke the news that Hillary had registered her email address the same day her confirmation hearings for secretary of state began. In other words, Hillary knew she would be secretary of state conducting official business, and coincidentally opened a private email account at the same time to guard her from Freedom of Information Act requests.

Sure, Hillary Clinton has a nasty history with crucial documents going missing—she is the only first lady in American history fingerprinted by the FBI, and the FBI found missing documents with her fingerprints on them in the White House personal quarters. But the media SuperFriends quickly activated to protect Hillary. Glenn Thrush of Politico tweeted that Hillary must have relied on incompetent staffers and lawyers. Ron Fournier of National Journal tut-tutted that this made her "no better" than Republicans. Of course, the media also ignored Saudi Arabia, the United Arab Emirates, Qatar and Oman handing millions to the Clinton charity just before Hillary's big run.

Clinton is hardly the first Obama administration official to utilize a private email account to shield herself. Lisa Jackson of the Environmental Protection Agency used a private email address under the name "Richard Windsor" to conduct official business. According to Vice News' Jason Leopold, the Department of Defense told him that they would not release any emails from former Defense Secretary Chuck Hagel, since "SecDef does not maintain an official email account." Other Obama administration officials using unofficial email accounts include former Health and Human Services Secretary Kathleen Sebelius and Donald Berwick, the former head of the Centers for Medicare and Medicaid Services.

Welcome to the most transparent administration in American history, where the Federal Communications Commission can regulate the Internet and keep those regulations secret before a vote, where top government officials can deliberately hide their emails from the public, but where your health records, income and emails are all government business.

The public and private spheres have now been completely reversed. The federal government can punish its own employees for enforcing federal immigration law; if you oppose this, you are a racist, but if you hire an illegal immigrant, you will be fined or imprisoned. The feds can monitor your electronic metadata, but they can hide their own correspondence from records requests. After all, they are our betters, and we must kneel before Zod.

What possible violations of the Constitutional system will Americans actually fight? The list of possibilities grows short. Reports emerged this week suggesting that President Obama will consider banning bullets by executive order, effectively castrating the Second Amendment by fiat. Shrug. The Obama White House announced this week that Obama was "very interested" in unilaterally raising taxes. Shrug.

Democracies die not with a whimper or a bang but with a shrug. When we don't care enough about the system to stop its breakdown—when we're happy with our dictators so long as we agree with them—the constitutional order collapses. But so what? By electing Hillary Clinton the presidency, we'll strike a blow against non-existent generalized sexism in American society. And that's far more important than having an answerable, accountable government.

Is Being Gay a Choice?

March 10, 2015

Last week, Dr. Ben Carson stepped onto a political mine—really, jumped onto it with both feet—when he answered a question from CNN's Chris Cuomo about the nature of homosexuality. "You think being gay is a choice?" Cuomo asked Carson, after Carson rightly stated that being black and being gay are two very different phenomena. "Absolutely," replied Carson. He then went on to explain, "A lot of people who go into prison straight go into prison straight—and when they come out, they're gay."

Carson's unstated line of reasoning is perfectly logical. When Cuomo asked Carson whether he thinks "being gay is a choice," Carson interpreted that question to mean: "Is homosexual behavior a choice." To that, the answer is obviously yes, since *all* non-reflexive behavior is essentially a choice. Cuomo, however, took his question to mean: "Is homosexual inclination a choice." To that, the answer is obviously no—it is either a byproduct of biology or environment. Feelings, in other words, are not choices; it is possible that some feelings can be shaped by behavior, but as a general rule, feelings are not chosen. Behaviors, however, are chosen. Thus, being black—a non-behavioral characteristic—is not like being gay or being straight, in the sense that one cannot choose not to be black, while one chooses one's own sexual behavior.

The divide between Carson's understanding of "being gay" and Cuomo's understanding of the same term demonstrates the rhetorical slight-of-hand that has marked the gay rights movement. By conflating behavior with feeling, and calling it all "orientation," homosexual advocates have conflated biology with choice, and called it all biology.

And even they know that such conflation is a lie.

Take, for example, supposed gay spokesperson Dan Savage. He understands that homosexual behavior is a choice. He compared being gay to being religious: "Faith—religious belief—is not an immutable characteristic." He also compared being gay to "military service and marital status." This is logically correct. But Savage refused to acknowledge the implications of this line of thought, because doing so would force him to recognize that society often discriminates between those behaviors it finds productive and those it finds unproductive in terms of the law (military service, for example, is a protected class because we all benefit from the military service of others; being a member of Code Pink is not protected, because we do not all benefit from someone's membership in Code Pink). Instead, Savage fell back on his trademark vulgarity, telling Dr. Carson to "suck my d---." "If being gay is a choice, prove it," wrote Savage. "Choose it. Choose to be gay yourself."

That is an insipid argument; were the shoe on the other foot, Savage would have to demonstrate that being gay is involuntary by engaging in sexual behavior with every male he meets. Given his prior solicitation of Rick Santorum, Mike Huckabee, and Herman Cain, that may well be his desire, but it's a rotten argument overall.

But arguments no longer matter. Logic no longer matters. Feelings matter. We intuitively understand that behavior defines us rather than feeling; no one would label a vegetarian a person who deplores meat-eating but chows down on steak every night. But when it comes to sexual behavior, we look to get ourselves off the hook: All sexual behavior is involuntary, so how can we be expected to make decisions about it? Hence the left's absurd lie during the Clinton era that everyone lies about sex; hence the asinine notion that chastity until marriage is an impossibility; hence the morally blind belief that societal pressure for sexual morality is discriminatory in the same sense that racism is discriminatory.

The result: No honest discussion can be had about the extent of human choice, the limits of human choice, and our own preferences among the choices human beings make. We are mere animals, forced by our firing neurons to act on each and every impulse. We have no choice. And those who say we do ought to perform oral sex on us.

The Charmless Hillary Juggernaut

March 18, 2015

Hillary Clinton is not a pleasant human being, by all available evidence. She does not convince; she browbeats. She does not discuss; she lectures. Her laugh issues mechanically from her mouth, resonating with a close-but-not-quite verisimilitude that occupies the space known as the uncanny valley. If anyone were to kidnap Hillary Clinton and replace her with a robot of Hillary Clinton, it would take a short circuit for America to realize it. Her campaign slogan should be: "Remarkably Lifelike!"

All of which makes her undeclared candidacy so much more awkward than that of others. Nobody quite knows why Hillary is running, other than that she feels she is owed the presidency based on her rough life growing up rich in Chicago, attending Wellesley and Yale Law before settling down as first lady of Arkansas and then first lady of the United States and then senator and secretary of state. Even Hillary doesn't seem to know. The runup to her campaign has been a prolonged shrug.

Which is why she is now trotting out the children.

First, Hillary's Stand With Hillary super PAC attempted to manufacture a grassroots feel for Hillary's campaign, issuing a faux country song titled "Stand With Hillary," and bearing these incredible lyrics: "Now it's 2016, and this time I'm a thinkin' guys, put your boots on and let's smash this ceiling." The song adds, "I've been thinking about one great lady, like the women in my life. She's a mother, a daughter, and through it all, she's a loving wife." A loving wife might be a bit of a stretch. But then again, so is a country song with men crushing the glass ceiling on behalf of an Ivy League elitist.

That song, naturally, flopped.

And the Hillary machine sprang back into action. A second pro-Hillary super PAC titled BillForFirstLady2016.com released an ad produced by Luke Montgomery, the same filmmaker who created a video featuring young girls dropping the f-bomb regarding supposed pay inequality. This ad features young girls wearing flag spandex and running down the street, urging Hillary to run (get it? Get it? GET IT?).

These girls then speak into camera and tick off five supposed reasons why people should vote for Hillary: to inspire young girls to overcome serious challenges like growing up female in the most female-friendly society in human history; to fight for pay equality by electing a woman who pays her female staffers significantly less than male staffers ("in the USA, having a vajayjay shouldn't mean less pay!" shouts one overproduced, irritating tot); to preserve abortion, which prepubescent girls desperately need; to show the world that female equality is a value, which we will presumably show by electing a woman who takes money from the world's most anti-female regimes; and finally, Bill Clinton will be first lady and "rock the dress."

The ad concludes with a man wearing a Bill Clinton mask, red heels, and a red dress. This, presumably, marks the first time that Bill Clinton has been in a dress that is his own.

If this feels strained, that's because it is. It is condescending, ridiculous, and—naturally—childish. But the charmless juggernaut rolls on, driven by puerile worship, empty bromides and a heaping helping of entitlement.

The Secret Life of Barack Obama

March 25, 2015

There is a unicorn lair in North Korea. We know this because the Dear Leader of North Korea, Kim Jung Un, tells us so. According to the official Korean Central News Agency, archaeologists have "recently reconfirmed" the existence of the unicorn lair dating back to the Koryo Kingdom (918-1392).

President Obama has his own unicorn lair. It is the world as it exists inside his head, Walter Mitty-style. In no way does this world resemble reality; it is a bizarre fantasyland of Obama's own construction, in which he is all-powerful, all-knowing and always right. It is a world in which his foreign policy predictions come true, in which his policies are successful, in which the flaming world he has helped create sparkles rather than burns.

In President Obama's world, Iran is not a threat, but an ally. Iran, in this world, is not an Islamic dictatorship, but a rational actor simply demanding the global respect to which it is entitled. The Ayatollah Khamenei's public statements of "Death to America" constitute a rhetorical love tap, designed for a "domestic political audience"—presumably an audience to whom the ayatollahs must answer, despite the lack of real elections in Iran for well over three decades. Iran's repeated statements that it intends to wipe Israel from the map simply show that Iran requires more concessions, not less. Iran's open suggestion that snap nuclear inspections be ruled out of negotiations show it is untrusting, not untrustworthy. Iran's expansionist policies in Iraq, Syria, Lebanon and Yemen are all growing pains that can be eased by Western kowtowing.

In fact, in President Obama's world, Yemen is a shining example of American foreign policy at work. Just months ago, Obama used

Yemen as his paradigm of functional anti-terrorism; two days ago, Obama's press secretary, Josh Earnest, said that Yemen "did serve as a sort of template for the kind of strategy that we would employ to mitigate the threat from extremists around the world." Earnest claimed that the Obama administration's anti-terror policy in Yemen helped to "stabiliz[e] the country so extremists can't use it to plot against the West." Last month, the American embassy closed in Yemen, with its Marine guard evacuated without its weapons. Last week, the last American forces left the country, which has been plunged into full-scale civil war by the Iranian-backed Houthi militias.

But the real threat to global peace, in President Obama's world, lies with the quarrelsome Jews some 1,200 miles to the northwest. There, the democratic country of Israel has endangered its status as a democracy by failing to negotiate with terrorism-backing Palestinians; there, Prime Minister Benjamin Netanyahu, a troublesome Jew if ever there was one, insists that Iran, not Jews building bathrooms in East Jerusalem, represents a threat to global order. If only the United States could achieve some daylight between itself and the Jewish state, all would be well—even though Jordan, Saudi Arabia and Egypt have never drawn closer to Netanyahu, knowing that Netanyahu is a far better guarantor of their security against an Iranian bomb than Barack Obama.

Delusional dictatorship is a danger to regional peace. But delusional American leadership is a threat to global peace. Nonetheless, things are going swimmingly in Barack Obama's head. Iran is a regional ally, Yemen is a model of peace and security, and Israel is an incipient enemy. The unicorns still roam free, even if free people live in danger of chains.

The Fascist Left and Same-Sex Marriage

April 1, 2015

Last week, Indiana Gov. Mike Pence signed a law with the same name as one signed on the federal level by President Bill Clinton in 1993, which was co-sponsored by Sen. Chuck Schumer, D-N.Y., the presumptive next Senate minority leader. Naturally, Pence found himself on the wrong end of a partisan barrage from ABC News' George Stephanopoulos for signing that law the following Sunday. It sure is nice to be a Democrat.

What exactly does the law state? The Religious Freedom Restoration Act in Indiana states that "a governmental entity may not substantially burden a person's exercise of religion, even if the burden results from a rule of general applicability." That rule does not apply only if the government's action "is in furtherance of a compelling government interest" and is also "the least restrictive means of furthering that compelling government interest." If government does act against someone in violation of that person's religious principles, he or she can assert that violation "as a claim or defense in a judicial or administrative proceeding."

The law does not specifically single out same-sex marriage as an activity against which a religious person may discriminate, but it certainly holds out that possibility. Of course, that possibility is already inherent in a little concept we in the United States used to call freedom—freedom to choose how to conduct one's business and freedom to practice one's religion in one's practice of business.

Under a philosophy of freedom, the market solves the general problem of private discrimination, because if one person decides to discriminate against Jews or blacks or gays, he or she loses money and is put out of business for his or her trouble. Nobody has the right, under a philosophy of freedom, to invoke the power of the government's gun in order to force someone to provide a good or service.

That system is a heck of a lot safer for minorities than a system by which government regulates the proper conduct of voluntary activities. Black Americans should know that, given that Jim Crow was not merely a system of voluntary discrimination but a government-enforced set of regulations designed to ban voluntary transactions involving blacks. Gays, too, should understand that freedom is far preferable to government-enforced societal standards governing consenting transactions, given that government used to be utilized to discriminate openly against homosexual behavior.

But the left has rewritten the concept of freedom to mean "whatever the government allows you to do," and leftists now insist that government cannot allow discrimination—unless, of course, the government is itself enforcing discrimination against religious Christians who don't want to violate their belief in traditional marriage.

Same-sex marriage, it turns out, was never designed to grant legal benefits to same-sex couples. That could have been done under a regime of civil unions. Same-sex marriage was always designed to allow the government to have the power to cram down punishment on anyone who disobeys the government's vision of the public good. One need not be an advocate of discrimination against gays to believe that government does not have the ability to enforce the prevailing social standards of the time in violation of individual rights. There are many situations in which advocates of freedom dislike particular exercises of that freedom but understand that government attacks on individual rights are far more threatening to the public good.

You do not have a right to my services; I have a right to provide my services to whomever I choose. If you believe that your interpretation of public good enables you to bring a gun to the party, you are a bully and a tyrant. So it is with the modern American left, to whom freedom now means only the freedom to do what it is the left wants you to do at point of gun.

Why the Left Lies

April 8, 2015

"When yet another hand clamped over her mouth, Jackie bit it, and the hand became a fist that punched her in the face. 'Grab its motherf---ing leg,' she heard a voice say. And that's when Jackie knew she was going to be raped."

Thus started a 9,000-word article in Rolling Stone magazine about the supposed rash of campus rapes across America. The writer, Sabrina Erdely, began with the horrifying story of Jackie, a college girl who found herself raped by seven men at the Phi Kappa Psi fraternity house at the University of Virginia while two other men, including her date, "gave instruction and encouragement."

The University of Virginia banned Phi Kappa Psi from campus. People vandalized the frat house, hurling rocks through windows and covering the premises with graffiti. Commentators and politicians all over the nation bloviated gravely about the deep problem of sexual brutality on campus. Those who questioned Jackie's story were accused of not taking rape seriously enough; to demand facts equated to shaming a rape victim.

There was only one problem with Erdely's story: It was false. Jackie had lied. And Rolling Stone had no evidence to back up Jackie's story in the first place. This week, Rolling Stone apologized for the story but did not fire Erdely or any of its editors; Erdely apologized not to the fraternity or its members but to virtually everyone else. She added, "In writing each of these stories I must weigh my compassion against my journalistic duty to find the truth."

Herein lies the problem. Journalism does not require sympathy for human beings. It requires sympathy for readers, who deserve truth. But for the left, truth represents a secondary value. It is far more important to forward a particular political narrative than it is to simply state the facts. And that narrative can only be forwarded if there is controversy over the facts. If, for example, everyone agreed that Jackie had been gang raped, there would be no controversy over sending her rapists to prison or prosecuting all those who looked the other way. But the leftist narrative requires an opposition, a group of evil haters who take rape less than seriously. That is how society can be blamed for the alleged rape of one woman by seven men.

So the left specifically chooses to feature situations in which facts are under dispute. Then leftists claim that no one could reasonably dispute the facts; the only people who would dispute facts about the occurrence of an evil are those who sympathize with the evil. Leftists craft Americans who require evidence into victimizers, simply so they can portray themselves as heroes. If you wanted evidence of racism with regard to the shooting of Michael Brown in Ferguson, Missouri, you were a fan of Bull Connor-style police brutality. If you wanted evidence with regard to Lena Dunham's rape accusations, you stood with rapists. Leftists don't require any evidence; they will take any allegations that support the narratives they desire at face value because that's how seriously they take rape, racism, etc.

The left's mythmaking will continue. And there will never be consequences for that mythmaking because like Sabrina Erdely, their failures spring from caring, no matter who gets hurt.

The Romance of Poverty

April 15, 2015

On Tuesday, CNN ran what should have been a puff piece in its travel section about the wonders of visiting Cuba. The title of the piece spelled out the angle: "Why you should travel to Cuba before it looks like everywhere else." The authors, James Williams and Daisy Carrington, write, "Cuba is not like other places, or rather, not like anywhere that exists today. To some outsiders, it looks firmly stuck in the 1950s. Vintage cars roam the streets, the landscape is absent of strip malls and global chains, and the buildings—though crumbling—hark back to a grander time." The authors conclude, "It is these throwbacks that lend Havana, the country's capital, an undeniable charm. A charm that, some worry, is in peril once the U.S. embargo lifts."

Who are these unnamed sources who worry deeply about the charm of poverty degrading into the soulless maw of capitalist enterprise? The left speaks of poverty with the same fervent attachment with which a lover speaks of his partner's quirks. Poverty is charming. Poverty ennobles. Poverty is Mimi from "La Boheme," Fantine from "Les Miserables," Che Guevara (the icon, not the mass murderer) and Gandhi (the icon, not the shamanistic wife beater). Poverty is artists struggling for their bread while crafting masterpieces.

And poverty is equality. Everyone calls each other comrade while they hoe their gardens for scraps of food. There's a real sense of community when everyone shares a general sense of hopelessness.

Most of all, poverty is wonderful—for other people. It's a great place to visit, but not a place you'd like to live.

But you need others to live there so you can visit.

And so the left romanticizes poverty. Primitive civilizations must be preserved, since they represent a simpler, deeper way of life. The poor rubes who occupy such civilizations must be kept that way for their own good, lest they be transformed into shallow husks of themselves by commercialization. John Smith came to America to rape and pillage for gold; Pocahontas stood for the spirituality of the mountains and the inherent value of the eagles. Only those clinging to the bottom rung of material existence can know the colors of the wind.

Now, it turns out that those experiencing poverty like it a lot less than those who look upon it from above with a wistful eye. Those Cubans who still hope to ride their 1959 Chevrolets to Key Largo don't see their throwback vehicles as a selling point; they'd trade them in a heartbeat for a 2005 Honda Civic and the ability to drive it to an actual job. The Cubans who inhabit those quaint, run-down buildings would likely beg to have Banana Republic buy them out and let them retire elsewhere.

But that would ruin the ambience. And so the left insists that Banana Republic stay out. Because, after all, the left appreciates the authenticity of poverty, even as they artificially create it.

Hillary's Vietnam

April 22, 2015

Headless bodies lie in the sand. Above those corpses stand the black-clad minions of ISIS, outlined against the coastline of Libya. This is the second video in three months depicting Islamic terrorists cutting the heads off of Christian captives.

Bodies float in the Mediterranean Sea, face down. Twelve Christian bodies, thrown from a rubber boat by 15 Muslims. Their launch point: Libya.

Approximately 700 more bodies float face down in the Mediterranean, victims of a smuggling operation gone wrong when their rickety craft sunk as it made its way to Italy. Its source location: Libya.

Four American bodies in Benghazi, Libya.

These are the wages of Hillary Clinton's war.

In June 2006, as then-Senator Hillary Clinton, D-N.Y., prepared a run for president, she stated that President George W. Bush had "rushed to war" in Iraq. A few months later, Hillary spoke of her opposition to Bush's surge in Iraq, stating that it was a "losing strategy." Iraq, a war for which Hillary voted, had been conducted on the back of flawed intelligence estimates and without a clear plan.

Five years later, Secretary of State Clinton rushed to war, allegedly manufacturing evidence to do so, and with no plan whatsoever for victory. According to The Washington Times, Clinton "was the moving force inside the Obama administration to encourage US military intervention to unseat [dictator Moammar Gadhafi] in Libya." Clinton claimed that if the West did not intervene in Libya, Gadhafi would pursue a genocide against his enemies; in March 2011, she imagined a scenario in which

"Benghazi had been overrun, a city of 700,000 people, and tens of thousands of people had been slaughtered, hundreds of thousands had fled. ..." That genocide never materialized, nor did the best intelligence estimates support that argument.

Not only that: Hillary also ignored all available evidence suggesting that the Libyan opposition was honeycombed with terrorists. She ignored Admiral James Stavridis, NATO Supreme Commander for Europe, who admitted "flickers in the intelligence of potential al Qaeda, Hezbollah." Al-Qaida backed the Libyan uprising. There was a reason that neither Hillary nor President Obama risked going to Congress for approval of the Libyan adventure: they would have been rejected.

Nonetheless, in October 2011, Hillary arrived in Tripoli to declare victory, stating that she was "proud to stand here on the soil of a free Libya." When Gadhafi was sodomized with a knife and killed two days later, she laughed uproariously on camera: "We came, we saw, he died!"

Gadhafi wasn't the only person who died. Hillary's war ended with terrorist chaos in Libya: a full-scale terror takeover of regions of the country including Benghazi, the exile of the legitimate government, a massive refugee crisis growing day-by-day amidst the upheaval. That refugee crisis has grown significantly worse since Hillary's war. As Vox.com, a leftist outlet, points out, 1,600 migrants "have drowned in the Mediterranean this year." Why? Again, according to Vox.com, when Moammar Gadhafi "ruled Libya, his government had an agreement with Italy to try to intercept and turn back ships leaving for Europe. ... And in the utter chaos that's engulfed Libya over the past few years, there's no government entity really capable of patrolling the Mediterranean."

Hillary Clinton's foreign policy has promoted chaos around the world. Nowhere is that better illustrated than in her signal foreign policy legacy, the collapsed state of Libya.

Ignoring Personal Responsibility Is a Riot

April 29, 2015

Hours after residents of Baltimore, Maryland, set the city aflame, President Barack Obama took to the Rose Garden to explain in professorial style just why America, under his administration, keeps watching young black men loot buildings and attack police officers. "We have seen too many instances of what appears to be police officers interacting with individuals—primarily African-American, often poor—in ways that have raised troubling questions. And it comes up, it seems like, once a week now, or once every couple weeks," Obama said, proclaiming that police brutality against blacks amounted to a "slow-rolling crisis." He added, "This is not new, and we shouldn't pretend that it's new."

Obama's disgusting implication was, of course, that a massive trend of police violence mirroring the racist police violence of the 1950s has broken out across America. That's false. Your chances in America of being killed by hornet attack are 1 in 56,000; your chances in America of being killed by a police officer if you are a black man are 1 in 60,000. Nonetheless, Obama continued by suggesting that police forces had to "do some soul searching," that "some communities ... have to do some soul searching," and that America as a whole had to do some "soul searching."

Fortunately, President Obama is here to heal souls, as Michelle Obama once assured us. And he chooses to heal souls by suggesting that all the ills of inner city communities crash down on those communities through impersonal forces having nothing to do with individual rotten choices.

"Without making any excuses for criminal activities that take place in these communities," Obama said, preparing to excuse criminal activities in the black community, "what we also know is that if you have impoverished communities that have been stripped away of opportunity, where children are born into abject poverty—they've got parents, often because of substance-abuse problems or incarceration or lack of education themselves—can't do right by their kids, if it's more likely that those kids end up in jail or dead than they go to college, in communities where there are no fathers who can provide guidance to young men, communities where there's no investment, and manufacturing has been stripped away, and drugs have flooded the community ... we're not going to solve the problem [with just police]."

This is cowardice. Impoverished communities like Baltimore are not "stripped away" of opportunity—they strip themselves of opportunity through lack of values. Children are not merely "born into abject poverty"—they have parents who get pregnant while in poverty and outside wedlock. Those fathers are not merely absent because of "substance-abuse problems or incarceration or lack of education"—they are absent because they make terrible decisions to do drugs, commit crimes, drop out of school and abandon their children. Kids do not just "end up in jail or dead" rather than in college—they grow up in an environment where crime is a way of life, and they choose to engage in crime. Baltimore does not simply lack investment because of cruel white businessmen; it lacks investment because no sane business owner would drop millions to place a CVS where the last CVS burned.

To blame a mythical white power structure for personal decisions that destroy lives represents an abdication of personal responsibility. Baltimore has a black mayor, a majority black city council, a black police commissioner. Baltimore hasn't had a Republican in a position of true power since 1967. America is not the problem. Baltimore is not the problem. The people who live in Baltimore and choose to pursue irresponsibility, egged on by big government advocates like President Obama, are the problem.

The New Lynch Mob

May 6, 2015

On Sunday, Democratic Maryland State Senator Catherine Pugh lavished praise on state's attorney Marilyn Mosby, who just days before announced that her office would file a bevy of charges against all six officers involved in the death of 25-year-old Freddie Gray. Gray's death drove protests and riots throughout Baltimore, serving as the spark to ignite local rage, and focusing national attention on the state of inner city black Americans. Pugh said that Mosby "really set the bar for the nation in terms of how these sorts of cases ought to be looked at."

Pugh wasn't Mosby's only conspicuous fan. Rep. Elijah Cummings, D-Md., who has represented the failing city of Baltimore for decades, said, "Her integrity is impeccable without a doubt." The widow of Eric Garner, the New York City man who died after police officers used a submission hold on him, said, "I feel like the same scenario that happened in Baltimore also happened with my husband. I would just like to see something done." Race-baiter and riot-stoker extraordinaire Al Sharpton stated, "We cannot keep playing Russian roulette on whether or not we get a good prosecutor or not." Crowds in Baltimore reportedly celebrated Mosby's indictment of the officers. The Huffington Post called her "objectively badass." Fusion called her "America's favorite prosecutor."

What, exactly, did Mosby do to earn such plaudits? She announced that she would charge the six officers, three of whom were black; she did so without laying out a compelling narrative supporting the charges brought (failing to buckle a seatbelt does not amount to either manslaughter or second-degree murder); she brought the charges while simultaneously pandering to the rioters, stating, "I heard your calls of no justice, no peace. ... To the youth of this city, I will seek justice on your behalf. This is a moment. This is your moment. ... As young people, our time is now."

If that sounds more like a campaign speech than an announcement of charges, that's because it *is* a campaign speech. Mosby was elected in January 2015 as the youngest district attorney in America; she reportedly has aspirations to higher office. Before her election, she publicly questioned the jury verdict in the George Zimmerman case and cast racial aspersions on the prosecutor who refused to file charges against Officer Darren Wilson (even Eric Holder's Department of Justice found Wilson's actions against Michael Brown justifiable). Furthermore, Mosby's husband, Nick Mosby, has excused rioting while serving as a Baltimore city councilman. Mosby's prosecution of the case amounts to a serious conflict of interest.

But even were Mosby not personally compromised by the political issues surrounding the case, mob justice seems to be running amok. When Sharpton, Cummings and the rest demand "justice," they aren't demanding justice: They're demanding the heads of police officers, without supporting evidence. In Ferguson, the narrative of the murder of Michael Brown trumped the facts of the case; Sharpton, Cummings and the rest still cite Brown's death in their litany of instances of police brutality.

Mosby's prosecution, however, elevates the lynch mob to legal status. As Alan Dershowitz put it, "this is a show trial." America has a lot of show trials in store, if the mob is to be placated. Marilyn Mosby doesn't care who burns, so long as social justice and political expediency are served. And the mob doesn't care what burns, so long as they get to hijack the political system to serve their thirst for vengeance.

Shut Pam Geller Up, or We Will All Die

May 13, 2015

Last week, Fox News' Bill O'Reilly announced that Pamela Geller, the woman who sponsored a draw Muhammad event in Texas, threatened America's national security. Geller, said O'Reilly, "spurred a violent attack." He continued, "Insulting the entire Muslim world is stupid. ... It does not advance the cause of liberty or get us any closer to defeating the savage jihad." On the same network, Juan Williams stated that Geller "engaged in gratuitous offensive behavior that led to the deaths of two people." The New York Times editorialized that Geller "achieved her provocative goal" with her "exercise in bigotry and hatred posing as a blow for freedom."

Geller, the narrative goes, should never have encouraged people to draw Muhammad because it was "provocative." To which the answer should be: So what? Women attending school in Afghanistan "provokes" radical Muslims into throwing acid on their faces, but that does not mean that women should not go to school in Afghanistan or be condemned for doing so.

Geller, the narrative goes, made Americans less safe by provoking radical Muslims, as though Muslims have no responsibility to act like decent human beings—as though, faced with the prospect of a cartoon of their prophet, Muslims have no choice but to grab guns and go a-huntin'. But that's nonsense. What *truly* spurs radical Muslims into violence is the well-evidenced belief that if they kill enough Muhammad cartoonists, soon people will stop drawing cartoons of Muhammad.

Geller, the narrative goes, was "Islamophobic" in her call for drawings of Muhammad; unlike Charlie Hebdo, Geller was not an equal opportunity offender of all religions, and therefore showed particular animus toward Islam. But failure to equally attack all religions does not make satire of one religion illegitimate—were that the case, The New York Times would have to answer why drawing Muhammad presents deep problems, but running simultaneous ads for the slanderous "Book of Mormon" musical is hunky-dory.

So, why the assault on Geller? The answer is simple: Too many Westerns have bought into the notion that personal responsibility can be jettisoned in favor of judgments about identity. Geller is the problem, in this view, because she is an upper-class Jewish woman from New York City; her rivals are poor Muslims from Phoenix. They are, by the nature of their identities, members of the victim class. She is, by contrast, a member of the victimizing class. Nothing either party can do can change their status in this equation. Therefore, according to Doonesbury cartoonist Garry Trudeau, even the Muslims who shot up Charlie Hebdo in France were justified: "Ridiculing the non-privileged is almost never funny—it's just mean. ... By attacking a powerless, disenfranchised minority with crude, vulgar drawings closer to graffiti than cartoons, Charlie wandered into the realm of hate speech."

How do proponents of this victim/victimizer identity dichotomy determine who falls into which category? They simply look at the socioeconomic status of those involved and make a determination of who is worse off. Thus, black Baltimore rioters were not people acting without any sense of values, but rather victims provoked by injustice from a non-existent white power structure in Baltimore. Before a conflict has even begun, we know who deserves our sympathy.

That calculus leads to more death, more destruction, more chaos. That death, destruction and chaos cannot be laid at the feet of Pamela Geller, but those who continue to perpetuate a narrative in which people who commit evil acts are victims, and those who are their victims are their provocateurs.

Barack Obama's 'Lottery Winners'

May 20, 2015

Last week, President Obama held a summit on poverty at Georgetown University. There, he explained that unrest in major American cities could be traced not to lack of values, but to simple lack of cash—and that lack of cash, he suggested, could be attributed to simple lack of luck. "The top 25 hedge fund managers made more than all of the kindergarten teachers in the country," Obama stated. "You pretty much have more than you'll ever be able to use or anyone in your family will ever be able to use. There's a fairness issue involved here." He added that we should confiscate wealth from those people and redistribute it to "early childhood education"—one of the greatest government boondoggles of all time—because that's "where the question of compassion and 'I'm my brother's keeper' comes into play. And if we can't ask from society's lottery winners to just make that modest investment, then really this conversation [on poverty] is just for show."

This is evil masquerading as generosity.

First, the simple fact that some people earn lots of money while others earn not as much does not implicate "fairness." Your earnings result from the number and value of voluntary transactions seeking your skills, services or goods. It is not unfair that those who understand how to manage billions of dollars on behalf of those who do not earn more than kindergarten teachers; there are far more people qualified to teach kindergarten than to manage money, which is why kindergarten teachers generally hand over their pension funds to money managers.

Second, Barack Obama's subjective view that some people have too much money reeks of monarchic arrogance. President Obama's net worth currently stands at nearly $7 million. He sends his children to the most toney private school in Washington, D.C. He and his wife enjoy taxpayer-sponsored vacations that would make Middle Eastern potentates blush. They also enjoy the favors of Hollywood celebrities who earn as much as hedge fund managers, but never seem to receive the same "you've got enough" Soviet-style central planning routine from the Obamas.

Third, President Obama should not invoke Biblical phraseology without understanding both plain meaning and context. Obama's own half-brother, George, lived as of 2008 on less than $1 per day. And when it comes to Biblical interpretation, the context for "my brother's keeper" comes from Cain and Able: Cain suggests that he need not watch over his brother shortly after killing him out of jealousy for Able's hard work and better sacrifice. Today's Cain is the modern left, which seeks to slay its brothers for the great crime of working harder and sacrificing more.

Finally, Obama's allusion to rich Americans as "lottery winners" insults the intelligence. Warren Buffett did not play the lottery. Nor did Mark Zuckerberg, Steve Jobs or Bill Gates. They worked hard, produced great products and enriched millions of lives. True lottery winners produce nothing; generally speaking, those who buy lottery tickets are disproportionately poor and spendthrift, and often end up broke again after winning the lottery. The only real lottery winner in this discussion is Obama himself, who has produced nothing and somehow lucked into the most powerful position on the planet.

America does not need wealth redistribution. It needs a values conversion. No poor person has a child out of wedlock thanks to the evils of rich people. No poor person drops out of high school because a rich person forced them to do so. Poverty can sometimes be chalked up to luck on an individual level, but it can't be chalked up to luck on a mass scale. And wealth can't be chalked up to luck, either. To do so is to impoverish our own values at the expense of our future.

Ann Coulter's War

May 27, 2015

This week, iconoclastic master Ann Coulter released her new book, "Adios, America!" The book has already been labeled racist by the mainstream left, which fears her argument, and will undoubtedly be marginalized by the mainstream right, which doesn't want to hear it. Coulter's thesis is simple: Since Senator Teddy Kennedy, D-Mass., rammed through the Immigration and Nationality Act of 1965, America's immigration system has transformed from a device for enriching the nation for both native-born and immigrants into a scheme for importing anti-American voters.

What made America America, Coulter argues, was a particular blend of Protestant religion and European civilization that led to the rise of the greatest nation in human history. What will unmake America, she continues, is a deliberate attempt to poison that blend with a flood of immigrants with wildly different values.

Coulter points out that the real number of immigrants currently residing in America illegally far surpasses the 11 million consistently put forth by politicians and media. That 11 million springs from census data, which is notoriously unreliable, given that immigrants here illegally typically don't spend time answering government surveys. The real number, she argues, is far closer to 30 million. And those 30 million immigrants in America illegally drive down wages, shred social safety nets, drive up the crime rate and congeal the American melting pot into a melange of inferior cultural values competing for local dominance.

"The foreign poor are prime Democratic constituents because they're easily demagogued into tribal voting," Coulter points out.

"Race loyalty trumps the melting pot. ... The American electorate isn't moving left—it's shrinking. Democrats figured out they'd never win with Americans, so they implemented an evil, genius plan to change this country by restocking it with voters more favorably disposed to left-wing policies than Americans ever would be."

And the Democrats have achieved their goals. America is more polarized than at any point since the civil rights era, and not by chance. Americans have been told that they have a responsibility to anyone who wants to enter the country, even as they are lectured that it would be gauche for them to ask just who wants to come in. "At what point will Americans remind their government that it has a responsibility to us, not to every sad person in the world?" Coulter laments.

The answer, if the left has its way: never. Bearing nostrums like "diversity is our strength" and "through no fault of their own," Democrats will browbeat Americans into accepting the demise of American values. The shock isn't that millions of foreigners want to get into the United States—that's always been true. The shock isn't even that Democrats want to open the floodgates to unchecked, unscreened immigration—that's been true for decades, given that the modern American left despises founding philosophy and the capitalist system more generally. The shock is that so many conservatives have capitulated, granted the left's premise in the hopes that America's new immigrants will resemble her old immigrants, even though the America that welcomes them has changed dramatically.

Coulter's argument—that the media and our politicians conspire to keep information from us about the effects of mass immigration from non-Western countries, and that such immigration will destroy the fabric of the country—is virtually unassailable. The only question left: Who will stand up to the tidal wave of political correctness to pursue a reasonable and sane immigration policy, rather than the insane combination of ignorance and bullying that currently dictates who gets to live in and help redefine the greatest country in the history of mankind?

Left Exploits Mental Illness to Push PC Agenda

June 3, 2015

My grandfather was deeply mentally ill. He spent nearly a year in a psychiatric institution after being diagnosed with bipolar disorder; he heard the radio talking to him. He became suicidal. He spent years battling the condition, until he was prescribed lithium. For the next several decades, the medication brought his mental illness under control.

Nothing would have been crueler to my grandfather than had society told him that his delusions were correct—that the radio was, in fact, talking to him; that the curtains were indeed threatening him; that he was normal, and that it was the stereotypes of the world inducing his paranoia.

Yet that is the view of the anti-science left that this week declared former Olympic champion Bruce Jenner a woman. Vanity Fair led the way, featuring Jenner wearing a one-piece corset, Photoshopped and made up beyond nearly all recognition. The 22-page profile of Jenner insists that everyone call him Caitlyn, addresses him as "she," and explains that despite the fact that Jenner has all male genitalia and all male genetics, he is in fact a woman— even though the writer explains his own confusion as to gender pronoun usage.

Jenner freely admits that he had doubts right after having his face surgically altered in a 10-hour procedure, but that a counselor from the Los Angeles Gender Center explained it was just the painkillers talking (it would be illegal in California for a counselor to explain to Jenner that he requires serious mental illness treatment beyond bodily mutilation). Jenner also admits that he is doing a reality television show about his sex change for the money: "I'm not doing it for money. ... If I can make a dollar, I certainly am not stupid. [I have] house payments and all that kind of stuff."

It's cruel to allow a mentally ill person to exploit himself in public, but the political left is happy to do so in order to perpetuate the pseudo-scientific nonsense that a man can magically turn into a woman. Their agenda: If men and women are the same but for hormone therapy, implants and repeated surgical intervention, then all disparities between male and female can be attributed to societal biases. And those societally created "gender constructs" can be corrected only by massive government intervention, including re-education of children. Bruce Jenner is merely a tool in this quest for redefinition of gender.

Thus, the White House hailed Jenner as a hero, with presidential advisor Valerie Jarrett tweeting, "Nice to meet you, @Caitlyn_Jenner. The brave choice to live as your authentic self is a powerful example to so many." Except that Caitlyn certainly isn't Jenner's "authentic self," any more than the "authentic self" of an anorexic requires constant liposuction. Surgery is not the solution to mental illness. The post-surgical suicide rate among transgenders remains 20 times higher than that of the general population.

As Dr. Paul McHugh, former psychiatrist in chief at Johns Hopkins Hospital, wrote last year, "'Sex change' is biologically impossible. People who undergo sex-reassignment surgery do not change from men to women or vice versa. Rather, they become feminized men or masculinized women. Claiming that this is civil-rights matter and encouraging surgical intervention is in reality to collaborate with and promote a mental disorder."

And promoting mental disorders hurts no one more than those who suffer from such disorders. Delusions ought not be supported, let alone celebrated. They ought to be treated.

The Right Caves on Social Issues, Then Loses

June 11, 2015

This week, a Wall Street Journal/NBC News poll showed a significant drop in the number of Americans identifying as conservative, and a significant rise in the number of Americans identifying as liberal. As the Journal described, "For the first time since 2010, conservatives are no longer a plurality: 38 percent identify as moderates, compared with 33 percent who identify as conservative and 26 percent as liberal." The Journal, like Gallup, attributes the drop in conservative identification to increased allegiance to leftist social positions, particularly among young people and women.

Predictably enough, the Republican establishment agrees with this analysis. For years, they have been claiming that the only path to national victory stands in de-emphasizing social issues and emphasizing fiscal ones. After all, as they point out, Gallup shows that conservatives beat leftists on economic issues by a margin of 39 percent to 19 percent. If Republicans simply drop social issues altogether, the logic goes, voters will be able to move into the economic realm, where conservatives dominate.

This analysis is dead wrong. It assumes two facts not in evidence: First, that conservatives can successful drop social issues without destroying their own value system and base; second, that leftists will ever allow a consensus on social issues.

First, Republicans cannot dump the value system that underlies conservative thought. Libertarianism is a fine philosophy of government, but a rotten philosophy of life. Without supportive social institutions to back responsible and moral decisions, free societies invariably crumble into the detritus of their own bad decision-making, and then call for the collective to help. Agreeing to an unwritten social contract of self-sufficiency is all well and good, until someone breaks the pact. And in the absence of religious and moral institutions outside government, somebody always breaks the pact.

Second, leftists will never allow a consensus on social issues. The entire goal of the left, in fact, is to promise consensus, then move the goalposts. Like Charlie Brown aiming to kick Lucy's football, conservatives constantly trust that they will be able to reach an accommodation with the social left. Meanwhile, the social left constantly destroys another heretofore well-accepted social consensus in the interest of casting conservatives as unfeeling.

To that end, the social left called for feminism, defining the movement as the ability of women to work freely; the right agreed. The left quickly redefined feminism to include abortion, the labeling of marriage as a patriarchal institution, and the destruction of any traditional notion of biological sex; the right disagreed. The left labeled the right anti-feminist.

Similarly, the social left called for deregulation of sexual activity; the right conceded. The left quickly redefined deregulation to include special legal protections for homosexuality, then moved on to same-sex marriage, and now pushes for legal measures against religious businesses and institutions. When the right disagrees, the left labels the right intolerant and homophobic.

All of this destroys political debate and conversation in order to label the right bigoted and nasty. And the right buys into the asinine idea that should they concede to the latest cause celebre, finally they'll have taken social issues off the table. And so the right goes from loss to loss, constantly bewildered as to why leftists keep winning even though the right keeps moving left on social issues.

The real answer would be to fight. If conservatism rests on certain basic notions of morality, that morality cannot be jettisoned in the quixotic search for electoral majorities. Those electoral majorities will never materialize so long as the right runs from its own values, tacitly conceding to the left the moral high ground.

Yes, Rachel Dolezal Is Black

June 17, 2015

This week, Rachel Dolezal, the former local head of the Spokane NAACP, a lecturer in Africana studies at Eastern Washington University, and a proud black woman, was revealed to be a non-proud white woman. She lied about her personal history: She said her parents whipped her when they lived in South Africa, that she underwent rape and physical abuse, that the KKK targeted her with swastikas and nooses. No evidence exists to support any of this. Her parents point out that Dolezal has no black ancestry, and grew up in a Montana home as the child of two white parents.

Nonetheless, Dolezal insists she is black. "I was drawing self-portraits with the brown crayon instead of the peach crayon, and black curly hair," she said to Today. "It's a little more complex than me identifying as black or answering a question of, are you black or white?"

Just two weeks ago, the world went gaga over Bruce Jenner's transformation into Caitlyn Jenner; the left passionately insisted that Jenner's genetics, hormones and penis did not mean he could not be a woman. The president of the United States felt the need to tweet out his support for Jenner, stating, "It takes courage to share your story." Anyone who abided by the antiquated notion that biological sex exists was treated as a Neanderthal holdover.

Now, however, the left insists that Rachel Dolezal is not black. On June 9, The Daily Beast headlined, "Caitlyn Jenner Is Pissing Off Feminists and Bigots—Good for Her." Three days later, The Daily Beast headlined, "BREAKING: NAACP 'Stands Behind' Fake Black Woman." The left insists on preserving non-biological, illegitimate racial barriers because they exploit those racial barriers for political gain; the left insists on destroying biologically based sexual differences because they wish to overthrow all established sexual mores.

So what distinguishes Jenner from Dolezal? On what basis can we reject Dolezal's blackness, given that the left has now redefined objective reality as self-definition? If you want to be a woman, you are a woman. If you want to be black, why can't you be black?

Nick Gillespie of Reason magazine makes the odd argument that Jenner had transformed into a woman because Jenner sincerely believes that he has transformed into a woman, whereas Dolezal had fraudulently lied about her race for gain. Now that Dolezal has averred her sincerity, presumably she is black.

Or perhaps there is some objective measure of race? But that, too, fails on the merits: Sex is significantly more biological than race, and it is significantly more significant than race. Skin color is surely biological, but the relevance of race is purely sociological, as even those on the left acknowledge. As Ian Haney Lopez of U.C. Berkeley writes, biology "refutes the supposition that racial divisions reflect fundamental genetic differences." Black people have black skin, but how black must your skin be for you to be legitimately black? In the Old South, one drop of black blood made you black, and therefore fit for discrimination. But that was a racist societal distinction, not a biologically based one. As Rachel Dolezal puts it, if you go far back enough, "we're all from the African continent."

Perhaps race is a societal construct and can change, but society must uphold racial differences for some greater goal? But that would be pure racism: The goal of fighting racism would be to alleviate racial distinctions, which have no behavioral basis, despite the musings of the would-be comedians at #AskRachelDolezal.

And so we come to this inescapable conclusion: By the left's standards, Rachel Dolezal is black. She can choose her race, just as Bruce Jenner can choose his sex. And she didn't choose. She always felt that way. After all, no one would choose to be black, just as no one would choose to be gay—blacks are so put upon in American society that no one would fake being black for, say, the benefits of employment or mainstream leftist celebration.

Perhaps we can all learn from Rachel Dolezal: Race doesn't matter. Except that it does for people like Rachel Dolezal, which is why she went black. Rachel Dolezal is a poster child for the deconstructionist, victim-manufacturing left. But now she's learning: Once you go black, the left will make you go back.

Confederate Flag Controversy
a Complete Misdirect

June 24, 2015

Last week, evil racist terrorist Dylann Storm Roof shot nine innocent black members of the Emanuel African Methodist Episcopal Church in Charleston, South Carolina. Before their bodies had cooled, President Obama attempted to blame the shootings on the National Rifle Association and lack of gun control; Hillary Clinton blamed the shootings on white supremacy and Donald Trump-like overheated rhetoric; Bill Maher blamed Fox News, and suggested that Fox News ought to be droned like al-Qaida propagandist Anwar Al-Awlaki.

Despite these divisive tactics, Americans united. There were no racial lines to grief: Thousands of blacks and whites marched in Charleston, packed the devastated church, mourned together.

But the American left could not stand such racial unity—it threatens their cherished belief that America continues to represent racial oppression and white supremacy. And so the media and politicians on the left manufactured a racial controversy over the Confederate flag.

Now, there are plenty of excellent reasons to oppose the placement of the Confederate flag on state grounds: The Union won, as it should have; the Confederate battle flag originally represented a new nation founded on reverence for slavery, a deeply evil institution; the Confederate battle flag was utilized by Southern Democrats as a symbol of resistance to federal desegregation during the Jim Crow era. Blacks in America are absolutely right to feel offended by the flag.

By the same token, there are plenty of decent reasons for the Confederate battle flag to stay on longstanding state monuments: to remind viewers of the fact that evil and good live together in every human heart; to remind viewers of the fact that good people did sacrifice on behalf of their states' sovereignty, not merely to defend slavery (most of those who fought and died for the Confederacy did not hold slaves); as a symbol of Southern military heritage, given that the South has always been overrepresented in terms of its military service in the United States.

My own personal belief is that the flag should not be displayed on state grounds, but is perfectly appropriate for display at war memorials. A country and state willing to remove the Confederate flag do not need to do so; a country and state willing to acknowledge their legacy of slavery and racism need not discard their history or monuments acknowledging that history.

Having a national conversation about what to do with Confederate flags and war memorials raises interesting and vital issues. But that conversation has nothing to do with the shooting of black Americans in South Carolina. The left's implication that those who revere the Confederate flag are all budding Dylann Storm Roofs, or that they sympathize with Dylann Storm Roof, is nasty and unsupported by evidence.

It is, however, politically effective. The left's decision to politicize the South Carolina shootings by immediately swiveling to a longstanding racial controversy demonstrates their sick inability to allow America to move beyond racial divides. Every conservative in America called for Roof to fry. That wasn't enough for the left—the same left that defends rioters in Ferguson, Missouri, and Baltimore and hero-worships Che Guevara and Mumia Abu Jamal. That left generated conflict because without racial conflict, it cannot survive as a viable political movement. And for the left, politics trumps American unity every time.

The Real Goal of the Same-Sex Marriage Movement

July 1, 2015

Late last week, after the Supreme Court of the United States declared without any Constitutional basis that the Constitution mandates same-sex marriages be state legitimized across the nation, a disquieting level of triumphalism broke out from coast to coast. The president shined lights representing the gay pride rainbow flag on the White House—a gross boot-on-the-throat display from an anti-religious leader. Corporations, undoubtedly fearful of the consequences of ending up on the wrong side of the riotous left, began tweeting out rainbow symbols. News outlets similarly embraced the rainbow symbol, as though it were uncontroversial to do so; BuzzFeed, Huffington Post, and Mashable all turned their logos rainbow, with BuzzFeed's Ben Smith explaining, "We firmly believe that for a number of issues, including civil rights, women's rights, anti-racism, and LGBT equality, there are not two sides."

Let's move beyond the romantically idiotic language of Justice Kennedy's decision. The notion that gay rights advocates and their allies, who have spent decades suggesting that the institution of marriage represents patriarchal oppression, love and respect marriage so much that they wish to join in its binds, is inane. And the idea that the gay rights movement desperately seeks the tax assistance available to male-female married couples was made false long ago with the promises of civil unions.

No, the gay rights movement and the broader American left celebrated the same-sex marriage decision in wild fashion because the decision established two fundamental notions: First, that government has replaced God in the moral pantheon of the United

States; second, that the new god-government has the power to root out and destroy any God-based institutions, destroying the social capital and fabric that holds together the nation.

The emotion that greeted Justice Kennedy's decision reeks of religious fervor. In ancient Israel, the Jews cheered ecstatically each Yom Kippur when the High Priest emerged from the Holy of Holies; that signified God's acceptance of the repentance of the people. This weekend's Dionysian displays mirrored that sort of delirious jubilation with Justice Kennedy as a stand-in for God: He declared the fundamental morality of homosexuality, not merely its legality. Kennedy went so far as to declare that the government could confer "dignity" on relationships. Now, the notion that the gay rights movement seeks the "dignity" of marriage is similarly ridiculous—movements that seek "dignity" do not hold parades featuring the Seattle Sisters of Perpetual Indulgence and a bevy of chaps in assless chaps. But they do seek the "dignity" of being told by a higher authority that their actions are right, just and good.

With God safely shunted to the side in favor of Justice Kennedy, the next step in the gay rights movement will be the smashing of idolators—namely, those who cling to their religion and church in spite of Justice Kennedy's New New Testament. Leftists have already moved to ban nonprofit status for religious institutions that refuse to acknowledge same-sex marriages; leftists have already sued into oblivion religious business owners who refuse to participate in same-sex weddings. It will not stop there. Religious schools will be targeted. Then, so will homeschooling programs. The secular religion of the left has been set free to pursue its own crusade against the infidel.

Religious institutions were the key social glue binding Americans together; we trust one another because we share values, beliefs and social institutions with them. With all three of those elements being memory-holed by the government in favor of self-expression, social capital will disintegrate; our trust in each other will fall apart, and government will fill the gap. With this week's judicial tyranny, leftists move one step closer to their ultimate goal, as expressed at the 2012 Democratic National Convention: "Government is the only thing we all belong to." And that will be an ugly America indeed.

The Most Idiotic Comment in Presidential History

July 8, 2015

On Monday, President Obama spoke about his new strategy to take on the terrorist entity Islamic State in Iraq and Syria. In doing so, he explained that the battle against that terrorist group—a group he had once termed "JV"—would amount to a "generational struggle." Why would defeating a ragtag army of primitives take generations? Because, Obama explained, "This is not simply a military effort. Ideologies are not defeated by guns. They're defeated with better ideas." To cap off this airsickness bag of gobbledygook, Obama then concluded, "We will never be at war with Islam."

So let's get this straight. A group Obama said he would degrade and destroy can only be degraded and destroyed with ideas. Its own ideologies—its animating force, according to Obama—have nothing to do with Islam. The cretinism here resembles a perfect Jenga tower of fatuity: Remove one phrase, and the whole structure tumbles.

Americans should gawk at the sheer wonder of Obama's applesauce here. Obama's bad acid trip bumper sticker foreign policy—"Better Ideas Beat Bad Ideologies" over a Grateful Dead peace symbol—reeks of third grade oral presentations. It takes more than great ideas to beat ideologies—it takes heavy weaponry. The victims of the Holocaust didn't sit around thinking to themselves, "Golly, if only we'd been able to come up with a better idea than Nazism, that Hitler sure would have stopped all this nonsense." America didn't end World War II by dropping informational leaflets. We dropped warning leaflets, then bombs. Large ones. Atomic ones. No armed ideologues in history have been defeated solely by better ideas—at least not before decades of murder, repression and evil.

So what did Obama actually mean? It simply lacks credibility to read the president's comments at face value: No sentient human being could be this dull. He meant that ideologies aren't defeated by American guns, because American guns are backed by American ideas. And American ideas are by nature bad, evil, racist, xenophobic, homophobic, centophobic, and, presumably, arachnophobic. Sure, American ideas backed with guns won World War II—but hey, pretty much any ideas backed with guns would have defeated Nazism, amirite? (Well, except for the ideas of the British, the French, the Czechs, the Polish...)

When it comes to fighting the ideology of ISIS, however, Obama finds Americanism insufficient, since Americanism *creates* ISIS ideology through Islamophobia. That's why Americans with guns can't defeat ISIS, says Obama: Americans with guns *create* ISIS. Only internationalism can win the day!

So far, that internationalism has been a massive failure. Of course, internationalism is always a massive failure, because it isn't an idea, any more than "diplomacy" is an idea. Both are tools, to be used by those who actually have something to say, something to fight for. But President Obama despises traditional Americans who have something to say or fight for. They are the problem. He is the cure. And he would rather disarm those Americans and their rotten ideas than let them loose with guns against those who slaughter babies.

None of this should be surprising from President Obama. He's been clear about his anti-Americanism since "Dreams From My Father"; in that masterwork of falsely nuanced detritus, Obama lambasted the "powerful" for their "dull complacency and ... steady, unthinking application of force, of ... more sophisticated military hardware."

Give Obama this: He didn't lie to us. 66 million Americans blinded themselves to his ideology, proving conclusively that bad ideologies are not always defeated by better ideas. Sadly, Obama's own rotten-to-the-core ideology continues to win victories, and the world continues to lose because of it.

Why Obama Turned Iran
Into a Regional Power

July 15, 2015

On Tuesday, Barack Obama championed his legacy-making agreement with the Iranian mullahs. That agreement provides billions of dollars to the Islamist aggressors hellbent on dominating Iraq, Syria, Lebanon, Afghanistan, Yemen, and any place else they can spread their regime of terror. In exchange, the United States receives a pinkie swear that the Iranians will not develop nuclear weapons for a grand total of 10 years; within five years, we will allow weapons embargoes against the state to end, and within eight years, we will allow missile technology to flow into Iran unimpeded.

This deal, Obama said, is a move in a "different direction."

He is right. It *is* a move in a different direction: America used to care when its enemies created spheres of influence across strategically important swaths of territory. President Obama used to pretend to care. In phraseology that now seems charmingly quaint, Obama stated in his 2010 State of the Union Address, "the international community is more united, and the Islamic Republic of Iran is more isolated. And as Iran's leaders continue to ignore their obligations, there should be no doubt: They, too, will face growing consequences. That is a promise."

Consider that promise broken.

America used to worry about its allies being targeted for destruction. Obama's new deal with Iran contains zero restrictions on their terrorist activity across the Middle East and the world, and relieves sanctions on figures including Qasem Soleimani, head of the Iranian Revolutionary Guard Quds Force, a group responsible for the murder of hundreds of American troops. The deal also enriches Iran massively, and Iran has made clear that it will use those increased resources to help its terrorist allies like Hamas and Hezbollah.

America used to fret about such things as the use of weapons of mass destruction—remember how cute it was when President Obama announced a red line with regard to Syrian dictator Bashar Assad's use of chemical weapons? Now, Assad can rest easy: His sponsor state just received the biggest influx of cash since the Iranian Revolution.

Neville Chamberlain could argue that in appeasing Hitler, he was trying to buy time to rebuild a crippled military in the face of an equally powerful force. Winston Churchill argued that Chamberlain's appeasement at Munich in 1938 sprang from a genuine desire to achieve peace and defend Britain. At least Chamberlain loved his country.

President Obama clearly does not. Unlike Chamberlain, he has purposefully hollowed out America's military, and fully embraces Iran's regional aspirations. Chamberlain didn't want Hitler to take over Europe. Obama wants Iran to take over large sections of the Middle East. Like most Europeans, Obama sees America and Israel as greater threats to world peace than Iran or North Korea. His top priority in the Iran deal was forestalling action by the United States and Israel. He achieved that, at the cost of Saudi Arabia and Egypt seeking nuclear weapons, Hamas reinforcing its position as a terrorist cancer in the Gaza Strip, Hezbollah retrenching as the controlling force in Lebanon, Bashar Assad ensuring his continued leadership, Iraq turning into an Iranian client state, Afghanistan preparing for Iranian-influenced sectarian violence, and Houthi-caused chaos in Yemen, for a start. But at least Israel won't drop a couple of bombs on Iran's nuclear reactors.

In 2007, I wrote of then-Senator Obama, "Iran's leaders must be praying every day that Americans turn to a candidate like Barack Obama." Obama's pro-Iran orientation was no secret then, and it is no secret now. Obama's Arab Spring has turned into his Islamist Summer because Obama wanted an Islamist Summer. No wonder America's enemies cheer the man 66 million Americans elected, even as the rest of the world readies for the inevitable onslaught.

Why People Like Trump

July 22, 2015

Last week, 2016 presidential candidate Donald Trump dropped his second headline-making comment of the race. Responding to statements from Senator John McCain, R-Ariz., in which McCain labeled Trump's supporters on immigration "crazies," Trump shot back that McCain wasn't a war hero, because he had been captured. "I like people who weren't captured," Trump said, paraphrasing a 2008 Chris Rock routine in Michael Scott-like fashion.

Trump's shot was mean, nasty, uncalled for, and idiotic.

The media world immediately declared Trump's campaign over. A few days before the comments, Huffington Post—a publication created by onetime failed California gubernatorial candidate Arianna Huffington—announced that it would feature Trump in its entertainment section rather than its politics section. The Wall Street Journal editorial board opined, "It came slightly ahead of schedule, but Donald Trump's inevitable self-immolation arrived on the weekend when he assailed John McCain's war record. The question now is how long his political and media apologists on the right will keep pretending he's a serious candidate."

Trump's rival candidates leapt on the opportunity to throw dirt on Trump's political grave. Governor Rick Perry, R-Texas, said, "I have no confidence that he could adeptly lead our nation's armed forces. His comments over the weekend should completely and immediately disqualify him from seeking our nation's highest office." Senator Marco Rubio, R-Fla., said, "I do think it's a disqualifier as commander in chief." Both trail Trump substantially in the polls.

Trump will, and ought to, take a serious hit in those polls after his McCain idiocy. But he will not go down this easily. That's because Trump exemplifies two qualities many Republican voters seek: brashness and an unwillingness to back down in the face of critics.

Trump's brashness is both his blessing and his curse—but unlike Spider-Man, Trump seems unable to comprehend that with great power comes great responsibility. He says foolish things, and then refuses to back down from them. But that stubbornness seems to act as a counterweight to his brashness, in an odd way: Conservatives hungry for an unapologetic candidate resonate to Trump, even if he should apologize for his latest tomfoolery. Trump puts himself in a position to draw fire from both the establishment Republicans and the media; when he draws that fire, even for good reason, the base leaps to his defense.

Even better for Trump, his long history of making inane comments means that it will be tough for any one comment to finish him. Like Hillary Clinton on the Democratic side, Trump is so flawed a candidate that it's difficult to tell where the fatal flaw may lie. In such a scenario, flaws become assets. Trump has shifted his positions? Sure, but he's done so constantly—he's a man of the moment, many believe, and thus we can believe whatever nostrum falls from his lips now. Trump has engaged in corrupt dealings? Sure, but he's so rich that he won't need to take payoffs, unlike those he's already paid off. Trump never shuts up? Well, at least he won't shut up when told to by those in power.

Upper echelon Republicans make a mistake in disqualifying Trump. Democrats never do this: Hillary won't call Bernie Sanders unfit for office, or vice versa. Trump will undoubtedly disqualify himself eventually, as well he should. Republicans can either learn from Trump's better qualities while discarding his worse ones, or they can try to destroy Trump as quickly as possible. The first strategy would be useful, the second wildly counterproductive. Unfortunately, as usual, the Republicans seem to be pursuing the worst possible option.

Evil in America

July 29, 2015

This week, the Center for Medical Progress, an anti-abortion group dedicated to unmasking the atrocities committed by taxpayer-funded abortion juggernaut Planned Parenthood, released its latest in a series of undercover videos about the organization. In this video, Dr. Savita Ginde, vice president and medical director of Planned Parenthood of the Rocky Mountains, calmly explains to the undercover reporter that the organs of babies killed in the womb can be sold separately. "I think a per-item thing works a little better," she tells the faux buyer while standing over a tray of kidney and spinal cord from a recently aborted baby.

The tape sounds like something from the laboratory of Dr. Josef Mengele. But to the left, the murder of the unborn is routine. Former secretary of state and 2016 presidential candidate Hillary Clinton defended Planned Parenthood, stating that Planned Parenthood has "provided essential services for women," calling the videos "an attack against a woman's right to choose."

Presumably, she then ran out of other euphemisms for the butchering of the unborn.

Meanwhile, former Arkansas governor and 2016 presidential candidate Mike Huckabee drew heavy media fire slamming President Obama's decision to guarantee both Iran's regional power and nuclear weapons within a decade. Huckabee stated, "This president's foreign policy is the most feckless in American history. It is so naive that he would trust the Iranians. By doing so, he will take the Israelis and march them of the door of the oven."

Huckabee's invocation of the Holocaust to describe Obama's facilitation of a genocidal anti-Semitic regime offended President

Obama significantly more than a similarly timed tweet from Ayatollah Khamenei containing imagery of an Obama silhouette with a gun to its head. Obama whined, "The particular comments of Mr. Huckabee are just part of a general pattern we've seen that would be considered ridiculous if it weren't so sad." Clinton said she was "disappointed and I am really offended personally. ... I find this kind of inflammatory rhetoric totally unacceptable."

She does not, however, find the prospect of a regionally dominant Iran lording over Iraq, Syria, Lebanon and Yemen, and building up terrorist groups like Hamas and Hezbollah, all while the United States provides a shield for Iran's nuclear program. The real problem, she and the left believe, lies in likening Obama's Iran policy to Western malfeasance with regard to Hitler.

The left's willingness to participate in Planned Parenthood's genocide against the unborn and the Iranian government's planned genocide against the Jews speaks to the nature of evil. Americans are fearful of invoking Hitlerian analogies because Hitler is seen, wrongly, as a sort of evil apart from the norms of humankind—he must have known he was evil, an evil of a different sort altogether from daily evil. The same holds true, people typically think, of the Germans complicit in his designs. That's inaccurate. Hitler undoubtedly saw himself as a good man. More importantly, millions of Germans joined in Hitler's evil because it was easier to look the other way than to confront the nature of an evil they had allowed to flourish. It is always easier to shrug through life by relying on euphemisms than to stand up to the daily evil we encounter.

For Planned Parenthood, as for leftists and their head-in-the-sand allies throughout America, babies are less than the sum of their parts. For the Obama administration, as for its allies, threats to Jews can be dismissed as irrational byproducts of religious fanaticism, rather than as core goals of an immensely barbaric regime. All of these accessories to evil convince themselves that euphemistic thinking will bring harmony.

Turning a blind eye to evil, however, doesn't make it disappear. It allows it to grow. And those who allow evil to grow in order to protect their own convenience will be held accountable for the end results of the evil they facilitate.

The Age of the Demagogue

August 5, 2015

Last week, President Obama visited the set of Jon Stewart's "The Daily Show" for the third, and presumably final, time. Obama has set records for the most late-night talk show appearances. He's also appeared alongside YouTube star GloZell Green, in the online series "Between Two Ferns," and Miami radio host DJ Laz, aka "The Pimp with the Limp." Obama has treated the White House like his own personal concert venue, complete with selfie-stick video. After all, as they say, you only live once.

Meanwhile, the same week as Obama's final French-kissing session with palace guard Stewart, Obama vowed to push through his support-free nuclear deal with Iran, utilize the power of the executive to curb carbon emissions from power plants and craft more executive action on immigration.

Buffoonish. Powerful. The two descriptors used to oppose one another in the minds of the American electorate. Now they go together like Oval Office and oral sex.

The modern media age has transformed our presidents into celebrities. When Abraham Lincoln resided at the White House, visitors could literally knock on the door and ask to see him. One European, shocked at such laxity, wrote, "one goes right in as if entering a cafe." Lincoln himself had to walk through crowds of people to get to and from his office. The presidency was the highest civil service office—emphasis on the service.

Today, we expect our presidents to treat themselves like royalty. Americans may decry the expense of the British monarchy, but the Kingdom of Obama costs far more. The president's family has access to the White House movie theater, with a 24-hour-per-day projectionist on call. The Obama dog, Bo, has a handler paid six figures. Overall, according to one estimate, the American royal family costs taxpayers $1.4 billion per year, as opposed to the crowned crew in Buckingham Palace, who cost British taxpayers a mere $60 million each year.

And like the British royals, our American royals are celebrities, treated as such. They hobnob with Hollywood celebrities, and even send their children off to intern with them. They shut down traffic in major American cities merely to appear on the telly. They are stars, not servants.

All of which would be fine, had they ceremonial rather than real power. But the president has unified star power with actual power. Early on in President Obama's term, my father noted that Obama seemed to want to plaster his face everywhere; he theorized that Obama used ubiquity as a tool, making himself part of the background noise of American life. That tactic worked not only in embedding Obama in every aspect of public consciousness, from sports (Obama's picking his NCAA brackets!) to reality television (Obama just congratulated Bruce Jenner on becoming Caitlyn!), but in making him feel indispensible. Obama feels far more like the head of a unitary, dictatorial government than he does like a cog in the machine of checks and balances. He bears more resemblance in the political optics to a Castro than to a Calvin Coolidge. We see him everywhere. And that is how he wants it.

It thus seems somewhat jarring for the media to decry the rise of Donald Trump, a reality television star long in the media eye. Trump, we are assured, is a joke—would we really want a celebrity as president? But Obama represents the apotheosis of celebrity as president. Hillary Clinton, too, is a celebrity attempting the White House—had she never met Bill Clinton, she'd be a screechier Barbara Boxer. There's a reason Senator Chuck Schumer, D-N.Y., doesn't merely spout his gun control views before the media—he trots out his cousin, "Trainwreck" comedienne Amy Schumer, to do so.

Perhaps the British have it right: a ceremonial head of state, and a politician to do a politician's job. Americans apparently can't handle a system in which our ceremonial head of state and our actual head of state are the same person—not without swooning at that person's feet, and offering as much power as humanly possible to boot.

The Extreme Party

August 12, 2015

During last Thursday night's inaugural 2016 Republican presidential debate, Fox News' Megyn Kelly got into a spat with Donald Trump over his history of vulgar comments about women. Trump followed up that tiff by dropping a thinly veiled reference to Kelly's menstruation in the media. Those comments prompted Democratic frontrunner Hillary Clinton to praise Kelly—a woman with whom she would never deign to do an interview—bash Trump, and then lash out at Senator Marco Rubio, R-Fla., whom she perceives as the most serious threat to her presidential aspirations.

"Yes, I know [Trump] makes great TV," said Clinton. "I think the guy went way overboard - offensive, outrageous, pick your adjective. But what Marco Rubio said has as much of an impact in terms of where the Republican Party is today as anybody else on that stage."

What, pray tell, was Rubio's great sin? He said that he believed the Constitution protects the unborn: "What I have advocated is that we pass law in this country that says all human life at every stage of development is worthy of protection. In fact, I think that law already exists. It is called the Constitution of the United States."

According to Clinton and her allies in the media, this makes Rubio—and any Republican who agrees with him—too extreme for the general public. And it's not just abortion. Polls show that 52 percent of Americans say that the Republican Party is more "extreme" in its positions than the Democratic Party; just 35 percent say the reverse.

But is that true?

On abortion, for example, the Republican Party platform states that the Constitution warrants protections for the unborn; the Democratic Party position states that taxpayers should foot the bill for the killing of unborn children at every stage of pregnancy, including partial-birth abortion, a gruesome procedure in which children are pulled feet-first out of their mother's wombs, their skulls pried open and brains sucked out. Then the Democrats want to fund Planned Parenthood to carve up those babies for organ sale. Which position is more extreme?

On same-sex marriage, the Republican Party wants to pass a Constitutional amendment to enshrine traditional marriage as the only governmentally rewarded form of marriage; until such time, Republicans acknowledge that same-sex marriage is legally a state's rights issue. The Democratic Party wants to force religious Americans to participate in homosexual weddings without recourse to the Constitution. Which is more extreme?

On health care, Republicans want Americans to be able to choose the healthcare they receive and pay for; Democrats want to force Americans to pay into a system from which they receive less than they would if they expended their dollars privately. Extremism, anyone?

The list goes on and on. Democrats want no major changes to the educational system, except for spending more money on corrupt teachers' unions; they also want to use taxpayer dollars to subsidize students majoring in useless subjects at second-tier colleges. Republicans want to allow Americans to keep more of their own money, and they want American parents to be able to spend that money as they see fit on the education of their children. Democrats want to dramatically increase taxes; Republicans want to decrease them. Democrats want no meaningful enforcement of America's immigration system; supposedly, Republicans want to enforce immigration laws.

Yet the media portray Republicans as the extremists. That rhetorical trick has its desired effect: Republicans are seen as nasty and unpleasant, even while Democrats move so far to the left that an open socialist is now their second leading contender for the presidency. Republicans counter by insisting that they are kind and generous, wonderfully moderate. This strategy is destined to fail. But

Republicans have no idea how to fight extremists, even as the left portrays them consistently as America's most extreme political party.

Straight Outta Solutions

August 19, 2015

Over the weekend, the hagiographic film "Straight Outta Compton" pulled in $60 million at the box office. The film follows the trials and travails—but not the woman-beating, gay-bashing, violence-promoting activities—of NWA, the iconic rage hip-hop group made most famous by their anthem, "F--- Tha Police." The theme of the film, according to reviewers, centers on the evils of the Los Angeles Police Department and white authority. Paul Giamatti, playing Paul Giamatti on steroids, screams at a group of stock-casting cops, "You cannot harass my clients because of what they look like!" He tells the group, "You have a unique voice. The world needs to hear it."

But while the world may hear this whitewashed version of NWA's nastiness—after all, Ice Cube now plays cops on TV rather than cursing them—the movie won't be seen in one place: Compton itself. According to CBS Los Angeles, Compton has no movie theaters. "It's a low income area, it's been heavily dis-invested in," says USC professor of sociology Manual Pastor. "When you live in a community that doesn't have that kind of retail, it's a sign that the community is devalued and people within the community feel devalued."

Compton doesn't lack a theater because of a feeling of victimhood. It lacks a theater because Compton overflows with crime. According to Neighborhood Scout, Compton's violent crime rate is 12.87 per 1,000 residents; chances of being victimized by a crime stand at 1 in 78, as opposed to 1 in 249 across California as a whole. The murder rate is reportedly 37 per 100,000 in Compton; the murder rate in the United States is less than 5 per 100,000.

So much for NWA changing the world.

NWA merely reiterated the anti-police propaganda that has kept inner city communities enmeshed in brutality and poverty for generations. Jill Loevy, reporter for The Los Angeles Times, describes in agonizing detail the lack of law and order in South Central Los Angeles, which covers Compton. She talks about how the police are underfunded in such areas, how witnesses are cowed into silence, how informal mechanisms of authority—gangs—fill the gap. "Residents would still holler 'One time!' at the cops," she writes. "The term derived from the memory of police touring black neighborhoods once a day, making no real effort to address crime. 'One time' was a stock anticop insult, just like 'po-po' and 'blue-eyed devil.' Yet it contained a plaintive note—a paradoxical suggestion that more times might be better."

The 14th Amendment to the Constitution, which contains the critical mandate for "equal protection of the laws," was designed to stop selective prosecution. The Civil Rights Act of 1866, the precursor to the 14th Amendment, explicitly stated that citizens— more specifically, black citizens—had to have "full and equal benefit of all laws and proceedings for the security of persons and property ... and shall be subject to like punishment, pains and penalties, and to none other." Leaving parts of America unpoliced, the Radical Republicans who wrote the 14th Amendment understood, placed them squarely in the lap of chaos.

Today, Compton's murder rate looks more like that of war zones than that of a modern American city. That's because any area in which no one enforces law and property rights devolves into pandemonium. Hollywood can glorify NWA; the Democratic Party can humor the counterproductive, criminal-glorifying Black Lives Matter movement. None of it will solve the underlying problem in heavily black inner city areas. Leaving black Americans at the mercy of lawlessness used to be a mandate of racism; now it's a mandate of political correctness. No matter who pushes that agenda, the outcome is the same: disaster.

Ashley Madison, Josh Duggar
and the Nasty Left

August 26, 2015

Last week, Internet criminals responsible for hacking the adultery website Ashley Madison released full records of those who registered to use the service. The media began perusing the list—and naturally, the first major name to hit the media was Josh Duggar. The media busted Duggar several months ago, too, when they released information that the former "19 Kids and Counting" reality star had molested children as a teenager.

What makes Duggar's infidelity noteworthy? The fact that he purported to be a religious Christian. In his adulthood, Duggar became executive director of Family Research Council Action, the legislative wing of the traditional family values promoting Family Research Council. He spoke frequently about traditional morality and traditional marriage.

The left media finds Duggar's hypocrisy on sexual morality absolutely delicious. The execrable Dan Savage, supposed anti-bullying icon, said that while he generally opposed "outing" adulterers from Ashley Madison—after all, adultery is a natural part of marriage, according to doorknob-licking Savage - that standard doesn't apply to advocates of Judeo-Christian morality. Savage wrote, "I feel bad for everyone who has been outed by the Ashley Madison hackers—everyone except Josh Duggar. ... Duggar—demagogue, liar, political operative—was a legitimate target for outing." Why? Because, Savage stated, quoting Evan Hurst of Wonkette, "he tried to hurt lots of people, because of how they have sex, which is why it is 100 percent A-OK to take this information and use it to grind that arrogant, fundamentalist pr---'s nuts into a fine powder so that we may snort it up and trip holy karmic balls." Delightful.

One of the great problems with modern American political and moral discussion lies in our hatred for hypocrisy above all other sins. Adultery, according to Savage and his anti-moral moralists, isn't a sin; rather, preaching against adultery and then failing your own standard is the great sin. But that makes all standards irrelevant. This logic sets up a perverse moral system whereby those without standards freely pursue whatever activities they choose, while those with standards are destroyed for their sins. The result: rational people choose to embrace amorality, secure in the knowledge that without standards, they will never be held to account. Bill Clinton can allegedly rape a woman and sexually harass several others, and he will never feel the wrath of the left: he does not promote sexual decency. But Newt Gingrich will never hear the end of his affair with Callista Bisek because he had the temerity to question Clinton's sexual peccadillos in the Oval Office.

The war on hypocrites isn't a war on sin: it's a war on standards. Josh Duggar may be an evil human being, but his evil springs not from the standards he attempted to preach, but from his failure to meet those standards. The left's backward obsession with Duggar shows *their* true hypocrisy: They violate all of their own standards in order to target someone with a different set of values. They are against outing, unless they want to utilize it to fight their enemies; they are in favor of adultery, unless it's convenient to use adultery as a club against their opponents; they're against sexual judgmentalism, unless they can use sexual judgmentalism to bash those loyal to Judeo-Christian beliefs.

Josh Duggar deserves to pay for his sins, and pay richly. He's vile. But those who fight against basic standards of morality don't have any moral authority to act as the agents of that judgment. For such jackals to play at such judgment smacks of the same hypocrisy they condemn.

No, the Democrats Don't Care About Israel

September 2, 2015

For years, the American Israel Public Affairs Committee has hosted President Obama or a high-ranking representative of his administration at their annual conference in Washington, D.C. No matter how anti-Israel the Obama administration's policies have been, no matter how hostile to Israel the president's rhetoric, AIPAC has offered President Obama or his lackeys a platform from which to tout their supposed pro-Israel credentials. AIPAC has always rationalized such outreach as an attempt to keep the pro-Israel position bipartisan, to cultivate supporters for the Jewish state on both sides of the aisle.

What a waste.

With President Obama's despicable Iran deal set for passage this week, with solely Democrat support, the Democratic Party has called the leftist Jewish community's bluff. Leftist Jews have played a sad game with the Democratic Party: They pretend that Israel's safety and security is their top priority, then make excuses as the Democratic Party moves more and more boldly to undermine that safety and security—because, in truth, leftist Jews care less about Israel and Judaism than abortion and redistributionism. Former George H.W. Bush advisor James Baker discounted the Jewish vote by saying, "F--- the Jews, they don't vote for us anyway." The Obama administration, with the Iran deal, has adopted a similar view: F--- the Jews, they vote for us anyway.

And there is no question that the Iran deal screws the Jews. Under the best-case scenario, Iran receives $150 billion immediately in unfrozen assets and oil money from the United States and her allies. In return, Iran pinky swears not to develop nuclear weapons. But they don't need nukes with all of the benefits President Obama just gave them. Iran wants nukes in order to use such weapons as a deterrent while pursuing terrorist activity across the world, preventing the rest of the world from leveraging sanctions. But now the rest of the world has accepted Iran's terrorist activities openly. President Obama's deal guarantees regional power to Iran—and then allows them to go nuclear with no consequences 10 years from now.

And that's the best-case scenario. Under the worst-case scenario, Iran grabs its money, funnels it into terrorism throughout the world, continues its takeover of Iraq, Syria, Lebanon and Yemen, and precipitates regional wars with virtually all of its neighbors. Meanwhile, Iran secretly builds a nuclear weapon—and Obama's verification regime does nothing either to verify or hold accountable. The deal contemplates a three-month delay between Iranian objections to inspections and supposed sanctions "snapbacks"—and even a "snapback" would require a new vote from the same countries now lifting sanctions, a dubious proposition at best.

The Democratic Party's latest kabuki theater involves allowing supposed pro-Israel allies like Senator Chuck Schumer, D-N.Y., to vote against the deal, knowing that Obama already has the votes locked up to pass it. Obama acts angry, Schumer gets to look tough, and Israel feels the brunt of President Obama's Jew-hating displeasure all the same. Meanwhile, leftist Jews get to comfort themselves with the idea that Democrats split over the Iran deal—and maybe, just maybe, President Obama has Israel's best interests at heart after all.

He doesn't. Neither do Democrats, or their leftist Jewish allies. President Obama's Iran deal will end in blood. And he won't be the only pathetic character in this drama with bloody hands.

Evil in America

Hillary Searches For a Heart

September 9, 2015

Hillary Clinton has now decided to re-relaunch her flailing campaign. She'll do so by showing "more humor and heart," according to The New York Times. In other news, the Wizard gave Joe Biden a brain and Bernie Sanders courage. The Wizard also apparently gave Biden and Sanders better poll numbers: In the latest Monmouth poll, Clinton still leads at 42 percent, but Biden picks up 22 percent and Sanders 20 percent.

That's trouble in Clintonia.

Clinton's new new new campaign will feature her dazzling wit and oozing charm, say her handlers. She'll be heading to "The Ellen DeGeneres Show," where Ellen will undoubtedly dance awkwardly with the former secretary of state—the most awkward dance since Clinton had to fake loving her husband for the cameras during the Lewinsky scandal. She'll also join Jimmy Fallon for "The Tonight Show," and "plans to talk extensively with several nontraditional outlets." Presumably, she'll head to GloZell's bathtub for a round of Froot Loops and foreign affairs.

It won't work. Clinton is like "Star Wars Episode I: The Phantom Menace": overproduced, heartless and starring a lead incapable of drawing sympathy. Some of her fans believe that if she trots out former President Bill Clinton, that will save the day; the Times reports that "Bill Clinton, who has had virtually no presence on the campaign trail, will begin to travel the country to help with fund-raising this fall." It won't help—Bill's spontaneity and glee undermine her in the same way that actual hardwood shames Pergo when the two are placed side by side.

Clinton does have a backup strategy: If Clinton can't overcome her status as the Tin Man, she can always go full witch.

Which is the plan, according to her campaign spokeswoman, Jennifer Palmieri: "The true game changer is when there's a personified opponent." She's hoping for a Republican opponent to emerge so she can pounce. Clinton is far more comfortable smothering her opponents with a pillow than cuddling with babies on the campaign trail. That's why Clinton has now placed heavy focus in her campaign speeches on attacking Donald Trump and the other Republicans: She's struggling to connect with Americans other than in opposition to those on the other side.

But what happens if she's unable to smear the person on the other side? What happens if she has to make an affirmative case for her own candidacy?

Clinton will be faced with that challenge if put up against an authentic, famous political cipher like Donald Trump, who now outpolls her nationally. Trump may be the perfect candidate to take down Clinton in a general election, in fact: He's not as susceptible to personal attacks, since everyone knows and has an opinion about Trump already; he's hard to peg down on policy, and actually agrees with Clinton on matters ranging from taxes to affirmative action; most of all, he seems like an unproduced person, rather than a remarkably lifelike robot capable of occasional homo sapiens-like jargon.

Over time, Clinton will likely grow more desperate—and thus, more unattractive. She's billing herself as Chillary Clinton in an attempt to seem like Cool Grandma to the under-30 crowd, but like an old PC, she glitches and freezes up regularly. Eventually, she'll run out of re-re-relaunches. The only question is whether the Democratic National Committee can wheel her to victory before other candidates catch up with her.

Rich Socialists and the
Bernie Sanders Moment

September 16, 2015

California is the land of hypocrites.

As I pulled into the parking lot adjacent to my radio station in Los Angeles, I noticed a Mercedes R500 sitting next to me. Between the Mercedes symbol and the R500 label sat a big, fat bumper sticker: "BERNIE SANDERS 2016."

The Mercedes R500 retailed at $71,000 back in 2006, when the well-off young gentledriver's parents presumably purchased it. Now, their kid pulls up to the pricey Equinox gym (sticker price: $160 per month) with a bumper sticker touting the virtues of redistribution of wealth.

This is the privileged generation of Americans. They've been able to benefit from the free markets of their parents; they can afford to purchase Fine water to sip while running on the world's highest-end ellipticals, then clean off beneath the rain shower head before heading out to brunch at Gracias Madre. Then, that night, they head off to the LA Memorial Sports Arena to listen to a 73-year-old socialist babble on about the evils of the system that granted them their wealth.

America has become so wealthy that its citizens now ignore the source of that wealth. "It's not all about the money" is an easy thing for rich people to say. But ask the billions around the globe living in abject poverty whether trashing a system that guarantees tremendous baseline economic opportunity seems like a great idea.

But this is what happens when no one teaches young Americans the morality behind the system that guarantees economic opportunity: young Americans decide that "higher morality" dictates the death of that system. Young Americans don't desire an Xbox and a car—they desperately want a feeling of meaning and belonging, none of which capitalism naturally provides.

Socialism, however, does.

The outcome: California. It isn't just the incoherence of bumper stickers and car brands that makes California the center of American hypocrisy. It's the fact that Californians routinely embrace more regulation and higher taxes in order to feel that quick boost of self-esteem, and then spend effort and time attempting to avoid those rules. Nannies expect to be paid in cash, because all the same people who voted for higher employer taxes refuse to pay those taxes. Young Californians only use free market Uber after endorsing higher minimum wage and more restrictions on transportation. Californians take massive tax deductions, but only after voting to raise their own income taxes.

None of this makes California more livable. Instead, Californians live in a fantasy world of their own making: a socialist utopia with a thriving black market, in which the popularly backed economy fails while individuals strive to avoid it. All of which runs fine, until the day that Bernie Sanders actually closes the loopholes and cracks down on the cheating. Then the Mercedes turns into a Yugo, and the bumper sticker finally lands where it belongs: on a product of socialism rather than free markets.

'Clock Boy' and America's Suicidal PC Tendencies

September 23, 2015

Last week, Muslim 14-year-old Ahmed Mohamed made national news after being detained by police for bringing a deconstructed clock to his Texas school. The clock, to inexpert eyes, looked like a bomb. Ahmed's English teacher thought so and called the police; when they questioned Mohamed, he reportedly stonewalled them. They released him after realizing that the device posed no threat and was not meant as a hoax explosive.

But this being Barack Obama's America, that didn't end the story.

The boy's father, a self-proclaimed anti-Islamophobia activist, decided to make a federal case out of his kid's detainment. He called his son's brief detention in an air conditioned room "torture." He called in the terrorism-linked Council on American Islamic Relations to protest Ahmed's treatment. When he reached the police station, he insisted that the police leave handcuffs on his son so that the boy's sister could take pictures. Then, when Dallas Mavericks owner Mark Cuban called up Ahmed to deliver his sympathies and began asking questions about the situation, Ahmed's sister fed him the answers.

None of those details made the press, however. The media simply played the story as a pure case of Islamophobia, a targeted attack on an innocent young Muslim genius who "invented" a clock. Never mind that Ahmed no more "invented" the clock than my daughter "invented" my keyboard by dismantling it. Never mind that children across America have been suspended or even prosecuted for far less than bringing a device with bomblike appearance to school. Form your fingers into a gun, and go home with the threat of prosecution looming. Chew a pop tart into the shape of a firearm, and you can guarantee it'll go on your permanent record.

But build a device that looks awfully like an IED, and so long as you're Muslim, the world will respond with outrage.

We have now come 180 degrees since Sept. 11. In the aftermath of that attack, we vowed we would not be hit again. To prevent that from happening, we told ourselves that if we saw something, we would say something; we also vowed to put political correctness to the side when it came to protecting safety. Now, we'll say something if we see something, unless that something is a suspicious act with regard to a possible explosive held by a young Muslim male.

When a 16-year-old black girl brought a science experiment to school several years back in Florida, she was arrested; Barack Obama didn't say a word, because she wasn't Muslim. But Ahmed now looks forward to a trip to the White House for breaking down an old clock and then getting testy with the police. This is America, post-frontal lobotomy. While we can all recognize and celebrate that Ahmed won't be going to jail, the treatment of Ahmed's case by the president and the press ensure that next time a young Muslim student brings a suspicious object to school, administrators will ignore it for fear of career-ending consequences.

And next time, that suspicious object may not be a disassembled clock.

The Republican Party's Big Choice

September 30, 2015

On Tuesday, members of the House Oversight Committee grilled Planned Parenthood head Cecile Richards over undercover videos linking high-ranking employees with illegal sale of fetal body parts. Under heavy questioning, Richards admitted to supporting sex-selective abortion, acknowledged that the vast majority of Planned Parenthood's nongovernment revenue springs from abortion, and awkwardly attempted to explain away the organization's alleged willingness to utilize special abortion techniques to preserve "samples" from the killed unborn.

That night, Speaker of the House John Boehner, R-Ohio, announced that he would fully fund Planned Parenthood.

Naturally, conservatives feel that they have been betrayed. Again. Since the 2014 elections, Republicans have done nothing to slow or stop Obama's historically egregious Iran deal, which almost guarantees Iranian regional dominance followed by their eventual development of nuclear weapons; Obama's executive amnesty program, which promises to continue to shape the country in heretofore unforeseen ways; and Obama's support for the nation's leading abortion mill.

On Wednesday, House Minority Whip Steny Hoyer, D-Md., said he looked forward to Boehner's last month in the House, and hoped that Boehner would "work with his Republican colleagues and with his Democratic colleagues to effect some progress on important things that we need to be doing." Hoyer added that Boehner "wants to get some things done that are important for the country to get done so that he doesn't leave that for the next leadership. ... I hope he can."

When conservatives hope the Republican leadership does nothing, and Democrats hope the Republican Speaker goes big, that's an excellent indicator that the Republican Party no longer represents its base. No wonder conservatives rally behind anti-establishment figures ranging from Donald Trump to Carly Fiorina; Texas Senator Ted Cruz draws heavy grassroots support for slicing Planned Parenthood funding out of the latest continuing resolution, even if it means Obama vetoing the CR, thus shutting down the government. Conservatives didn't elect Republicans to build a power base. They elected them to enact conservative policy preferences, no matter the cost.

But Republican Party insiders seem puzzled at the rage of the conservative base over their collective decision not to oppose the most controversial elements of President Obama's agenda. Instead, Republicans insist to their voters that they're doing their best, that without 66 votes in the Senate, they can't override the executive branch, and that they will need just a few more dollars, pretty, pretty please.

This conflict lays bare the conflicting agendas of conservatives and Republican leaders. Republican leaders believe the goal of the Republican Party is to gain and maintain power; conservatives believe the goal of the Republican Party is to represent conservative interests, no matter what comes. The Republican Party has become an excellent vehicle for the former goal, and a smoking garbage heap when it comes to the latter.

Republicans may keep winning, because the only alternative for conservatives is to vote Democrat. For now. But the divergence between the base and the leadership will eventually lead to the GOP's collapse, unless Republican leaders begin to re-orient themselves to a conservative true north.

Barack Obama, Jackass

October 7, 2015

Last week, in the aftermath of the mass shooting at Umpqua Community College in Oregon, President Barack Obama took to the microphones to deride anyone who did not agree with his gun control agenda. Stating that it was only good and right to "politicize" the Oregon shooting, Obama stated, "This is a political choice that we make to allow this to happen every few months in America. We collectively are answerable to those families, who lose their loved ones, because of our inaction." Obama then called for "modest" gun regulations, without specifying the nature of those "modest" gun regulations.

No one "allows" mass shootings to happen other than those who refuse to arm guards or give potential victims the ability to protect themselves. But that didn't stop Obama from using the deaths of innocents as a platform for his childish "DO SOMETHING!!!!!" antics. Obama specifically presented no gun agenda, because none of the regulations he has proposed in the past would have stopped an incident like Umpqua Community College. He implies that he's interested in full-scale gun confiscation, but he's far more interested in demonizing his political opposition, painting all of his opponents are mean-spirited and cruel-hearted.

That's because he's a jackass. Leveling personal accusations without a shred of evidence makes you a jackass, and Obama fits that definition to a T.

Now, he's not unique in this regard. Hillary Clinton recently suggested that Republicans who oppose Planned Parenthood resemble "terrorist groups" and that conservatives who oppose illegal immigration want to use Nazi-like "boxcars" to deport millions. Joe Biden infamously stated in 2012 that Republicans wanted to put black people "back in chains." Because leftist policy prescriptions invariably involve ignoring crucial issues in favor of feel-good incoherence, their main political play is name-calling sans evidence.

But Obama has perfected the craft.

The main problem with this tactic isn't its cynical political use— it's that Obama thinks it actually works. Hence, Obama's jackassery doesn't stop at water's edge. Last week, as Vladimir Putin pressed his advantage in Syria, Obama told the world that Putin presented little threat. Why? Putin went into Syria "out of weakness. ... I didn't see, after he made that speech in the United Nations, suddenly the 60-nation coalition that we have start lining up behind him. Iran and Assad make up Mr. Putin's coalition at the moment. The rest of the world makes up ours."

Faculty lounge insults will not stop Putin in Syria. And Obama's vaunted coalition is illusory: No one will stop Putin or Assad, including Obama. But Obama has become so convinced of the success of the Jackass Strategy that he uses it to no avail on America's opponents. Putin is not running against Obama; he's not Mitt Romney. But Obama acts as though Putin is somehow vulnerable to the same sorts of emotional blackmail as Republican opponents. He isn't.

We should be smart enough not to fall for Obama's jackassery when it comes to domestic politics. But America becomes more vulnerable when the president only knows how to insult, and thinks our foreign enemies give a damn about his sneering blather.

The Anti-Jew Anti-Gun Crusade

October 14, 2015

This week, 2016 Republican presidential contender Dr. Ben Carson bore the brunt of the media's ire for his politically incorrect take on the evils of gun control. "Through a combination of removing guns and disseminating propaganda, the Nazis were able to carry out their evil intentions with relatively little resistance," Carson writes in his new book, "A Perfect Union."

Leftists, including the activists of the Anti-Defamation League, promptly condemned Carson. National Director Jonathan Greenblatt explained, "the notion that Hitler's gun-control policy contributed to the Holocaust is historically inaccurate." Nick Baumann of The Huffington Post wrote, "There was some armed Jewish resistance to the power of the Nazi war machine. But it often ended in death for the Jews involved."

This is the height of idiocy. Pretty much everything ended in death for Jews during World War II in Europe. But what gave them a better shot of survival: having a gun or being completely disarmed?

Historically, enemies of the Jews—or any other subject population, for that matter—have sought to disarm the Jews in order to carry out their designs. This goes all the way back to the Bible, in which the Philistines banned all ironsmiths from the Jews, explicitly stating, "Lest the Jews make them swords or spears." Hitler knew the efficacy of gun control, and effectuated it with regard to Jews throughout his regime: While guns were completely banned in Germany in 1920, the laws were liberalized in 1928 before Hitler cracked down on Jews from 1933 to 1938, when full confiscation of all weapons, including knives, from Jews took place. The penalty for Jewish ownership of weapons: condemnation to a concentration

camp for up to 20 years. Jews were warned that "they should interpret the new ordinance and the already existing Weapons Law strictly."

Would Jewish weapons have helped prevent the Holocaust? They certainly would have saved more Jewish lives. Jewish resistance in the death camps of Sobibor and Treblinka shut them down; Jewish resistance in the Warsaw Ghetto led to over a thousand German casualties. Armed resistance is invariably a better method of self-defense against tyranny than nothing.

Meanwhile, in the Holy Land, the British sought to prevent Jewish weapons ownership as well, so as to prevent those uppity Jews from seizing control of pre-independence Israel. Jewish independence fighters, victimized by Arab gangs and British authorities who cast a warm eye on them, began manufacturing bullets underground and transporting them using milk trucks. After World War II, Jews were unlikely to surrender their weapons to supposedly friendly authorities. They didn't. The result: a Jewish State.

Guns matter. Self-defense matters.

The left wants Jews to surrender both.

Today, the world turns a blind eye as Palestinian Arabs stab children in the streets of Jerusalem—and they tell the Israelis not to worry so much about Iranian terror support or the Iranian nuclear program. Jews should simply stop being so militaristic, tell their armed citizens to stop fighting with terrorists armed with blades. Surely, that will end the cycle of violence.

But for centuries, the cycle of violence has not ended with regard to Jews. That's because there is no cycle of violence: It's a consistent pattern of Jew-hatred carried forward to violence. Denigrating Jewish self-defense means more dead Jews. More importantly, it means depriving Jews of their humanity. The first human right is the right to defend your life and your family, even if you can't win. More good people with guns fighting tyranny make the world a better place. That was true in 1944, and it's true today. That rule doesn't change just because the world seems indifferent to Jewish suffering, no matter what the era.

Superman Takes on the Cops, Batman Takes on Gentrification, and Captain America Takes on Border Control

October 21, 2015

One of the most depressing features of modern American life lies in the left's total war on every facet of our shared culture. It isn't enough to produce movies with Steve Carell and Julianne Moore and Ellen Page about lesbian partners seeking legal protection for conveyance of property. Now, even comic books must be hijacked in order to promote leftist messaging.

The latest run of Captain America features the newest Cap, Sam Wilson, taking on the Sons of the Serpent—an evil group of tea party types intent on stopping illegal immigration. The writer, Nick Spencer, is an ardent opponent of Donald Trump, and slathered the comic with his dislike for conservatives: the Sons of the Serpent amass at the border to stop the poor, bewildered illegal immigrants, whereupon the Sons of the Serpent leader announces, "Attention all trespassers! I am the Supreme Serpent! By invading this sovereign land, you defy the laws of God, Nature and the United States Constitution. Therefore, I hereby apprehend you by the power vested in me by the aforementioned God, Nature, et cetera, et cetera." One of the illegal immigrants cries, "Please, whoever you are—we don't want any trouble—"

But the Supreme Serpent will have none of it: he continues, "Until the mighty wall is built, you come here for employment that is rightfully ours! And if denied it, you seek welfare paid for by our tax dollars!"

Thankfully, Captain America stops by to shut down the Minutemen wannabes, shouting, "If you're done threatening a bunch of unarmed folks, mostly women and children ... I'd pack up the pickup and head home if I were you, gentlemen."

It's not just Captain America now mouthing leftist talking points. Superman, once a friend to the cops, has now become their enemy. In the latest run of Superman Action Comics No. 42, the temporarily powerless Man of Steel ends up on the wrong side of the police—a group of faceless fascists looking to shut down any discussion. That's when Superman arrives to take on the riot squad. That follows on the incredibly overrated Grant Morrison making Superman a black president of the United States back in Action Comics No. 9 in 2012.

And then there's Batman No. 44, in which the Caped Crusader stumbles on the body of a slain black teenager. The teenager was shot by a cop while wearing a hoodie. Writer Scott Snyder said, "Of course you want Batman to beat this officer up, and be like, 'How could you?'"

How did this black teenager end up in a confrontation with the police in the first place? He went to the Penguin for a loan since the evil, evil banks wouldn't give him a loan based on his lack of credit history; he needed a loan to keep his father's corner business going. For some reason, all of this is supposedly Bruce Wayne's fault for gentrifying the area—even though gentrification would make his corner business valuable, and therefore saleable. Writer Brian Azzarello explains, "This thing is such a ripple, the way lives are affected by gentrification. ... And if you have no money, you have no voice."

Culture is one of the few areas of American life that allows us to continue to speak with one another. Left and right may have little in common, but we all like our movies and our television shows and our comic books. But when the left decides to turn comics into yet another outlet for their political propaganda, those cultural ties break, leaving yet another, small gap in our common life—and indoctrinating another generation into leftist nonsense.

No, Hillary Didn't Care About Chris Stevens

October 28, 2015

Last week, the media hailed Hillary Clinton's supposed political triumph at a hearing of the House Select Committee on Benghazi concerning the terrorist attack of Sept. 11, 2012 that ended in the murder of four Americans, including American ambassador to Libya, Christopher Stevens. Clinton appeared calm and collected, even as she lied repeatedly: She said that she believed a YouTube video still bore some responsibility for the terrorist attack, despite the fact that she told the Egyptian prime minister the day after the attack that the video had nothing to do with the attack; she insisted that political hack Sidney Blumenthal didn't act as an advisor, even though he routinely emailed with her about policy; she stated that she'd been transparent about her emails, although that nonsense has been rejected by the State Department.

Most of all, Clinton suggested that Stevens had been responsible for his own murder. She said that he "felt comfortable" on the ground, and that he was merely joking when he emailed about whether the Benghazi compound would be closed. "Chris Stevens had ... a really good sense of humor," Clinton laughed. "And I just see him smiling as he's typing this." Stevens' State Department team in Libya sent requests for additional security 600 times. They were rejected.

After Clinton finished lying, she went home and hung out with her entire team. She partied. "I had my whole team come over to my house and we sat around eating Indian food and drinking wine and beer," Clinton told MSNBC's Rachel Maddow. "That's what we did. It was great. ... They did a terrific job, you know, kind of being there behind me and getting me ready, and then, you know, just talk about what we're going to do next."

As an apparent afterthought, she added to Maddow, "The point is, what are we going to do both honor and the people that we lost, and try to make sure this doesn't happen again."

Chris Stevens was always an afterthought to Clinton, despite her crocodile tears at the hearing, where she complained, "I would imagine I've thought more about what happened than all of you put together. I've lost more sleep than all of you put together." She didn't give Stevens her private email address, though Blumenthal had it. She couldn't remember holding a single conversation with Stevens after he was appointed ambassador to Libya. The night of his death she sent an email with the subject line "Chris Smith," mixing up his name with that of fellow diplomat Sean Smith. She spoke to survivors only days later. The night of the attack, she didn't speak with the Secretary of Defense Leon Panetta or the Chairman of the Joint Chiefs of Staff Martin Dempsey.

Clinton's aggressive case for the invasion of Libya led to the overthrow and killing of dictator Moammar Gadhafi—an event for which Clinton was happy to take credit, laughing, "We came, we saw, he died." She then completely ignored Libya as it turned into a terrorist hellhole, because that inconvenient fact undercut her narrative of strength and purpose. Her State Department refused to grant additional security requests because doing so would have implicitly recognized the failure of her war. Then, after Stevens died, Clinton and her team lied to the American people and the families of the slain, pinning the murders on an unforeseeable YouTube video-driven attack, rather than an utterly foreseeable terrorist attack.

Clinton is a coldly manipulative, deeply ambitious politician willing to say and do anything to achieve power. She was always that person, which is why she lied to Americans from in front of the flag-draped caskets of the murdered men in Benghazi. And she is that person now, too, as she laughs and eats Indian food hours after maintaining her lies once again before the American people.

Republicans vs. The Media

November 4, 2015

For years, I have been begging Republicans to stand up to the mainstream media. The left has dominated the media for as long as I've been alive. Yet Republicans have consistently granted leftists in media the patina of legitimacy: they've appeared on their programs, answered their questions without quibble, and allowed the audience to believe that the questions themselves spring from a place of objectivity rather than a desire to harm Republicans.

The political damage has been near incalculable. In 2012, Clinton and George Stephanopoulos singlehandedly redirected the presidential election narrative by asking Republican frontrunner Mitt Romney about banning contraceptives—a policy that no Republican had advocated at any point during the campaign. A few months later, CNN's in-house Barack Obama serviceperson Candy Crowley won the second presidential debate by wrongly telling Romney that Obama had labeled Benghazi a terrorist attack.

So why haven't Republicans fought back? Because Republicans have had a collective action problem. For each Republican willing to label George Stephanopoulos a political hack, there's a camera-loving John McCain willing to grant Stephanopoulos the premise of neutrality for a bit of airtime. For every Republican willing to ask CNBC moderators about their history of leftist questioning, there's a John Kasich willing to praise the moderators as open-minded and fair.

All this came to an end last week. CNBC, in its gauche attempt to grab ratings, set up a rogue's gallery of leftists, all of whom proceeded to berate, bash, and browbeat the various candidates into looking foolish. That continued until Senator Ted Cruz, R., Texas, put a stop to it: "This is not a cage match ... how about talking about the substantive issues people care about?" Cruz pointed out, correctly, that none of the questioners would be voting in a Republican primary—the implication being that the moderators have priorities other than asking honest questions. That started the pile-on. Senator Marco Rubio, R., Fla., jumped in and called the media Hillary Clinton's Super PAC. Governor Chris Christie, R., N.J., bashed moderator John Harwood for being rude, even by New Jersey standards.

And then the candidates came together and said they would no longer abide by rules set by a ratings-seeking, leftist media, and the ratings-seeking, donation-machine Republican National Committee. Instead, they would approve moderators in advance, and demand that those asking the questions be held up to a standard of decency.

The media, naturally, went nearly insane over this slight. Like pearl-clutching CNBC moderator Carl Quintanilla, who peckishly refused to let Cruz answer his question on Obamacare after Cruz slapped the media, the members of the media insisted that the real offenders were the intransigent Republicans. Then the Democratic National Committee announced that MSNBC host Rachel Maddow would be moderating a live presidential forum, humiliating that argument.

The Republican willingness to partake in its own political demise has undermined conservatism for years. Now the mask is off. Thanks to CNBC for that.

The Leftist Tree Must Be Watered With Blood at Mizzou

November 11, 2015

University of Missouri President Tim Wolfe must wonder what he did wrong.

It all began back in September when the black student government president complained that a racist drove by in a truck and allegedly called him a racial slur. Then, in September, a group of black students said that a drunken white racist shouted a slur at them, too.

Ugly, of course. But in any normal world, without further evidence of the incidents, life would have gone on—occasional ugliness from ugly people is a feature of living on Earth. But that wasn't good enough: somehow, Wolfe had to be held responsible, according to the student body. The election of a black student government president was less representative of the campus climate than a couple of shouted names. Thus, the radical group Concerned Student 1950 shut down the university's homecoming parade, then surrounded Wolfe's car and tried to force him to get out. When he refused and called the police, they protested him as a racist.

And, like a good little leftist, Wolfe apologized. "I am sorry, and my apology is long overdue," he said. "My behavior seemed like I did not care. That was not my intention."

That did not appease the baying crowd, however.

One graduate student began a hunger strike for no apparent reason. But Wolfe continued to scrape and bow before those who would have his head, saying of the would-be revolutionary, "his voice for social justice is important and powerful. He is being heard and I am listening. I am thankful for the leadership provided by him and the other student leaders in raising awareness of racism, injustice and intolerance."

Still not good enough.

The Concerned Student 1950 group released a demand letter. They wanted Wolfe to show them a handwritten letter—not typed, mind you—admitting his own "white privilege." Such privilege apparently included the distinct honor of being fired for his skin color while being forced to maintain that his position is advantageous due to his skin color.

On Friday night, a group of students accosted him at an event, reading him the riot act about the chimera known as "white privilege." He stated, "Systematic oppression is because you don't believe that you have the equal opportunity for success—" At this point, one of the students began screaming at him, accusing him of blaming black students for their own feelings of alienation. Which, given the evidence, would have been a solid accusation. But Wolfe didn't even make it.

Then, 30 black members of the football team—many of whom were on athletic scholarships provided for them despite academic underachievement—announced they wouldn't play football so long as Wolfe remained. The white coach of the team, who earns $3.1 million from the taxpayer-sponsored university, joined the protest. He was not accused of "white privilege."

Finally, on Monday, Wolfe resigned. He said, "It is clear to all of us that change is needed, and we appreciate the thoughtfulness and passion which have gone into the sharing of concerns." Such thoughtfulness apparently included shouting down members of the media and blocking them from covering protests.

But with Wolfe's career in tatters solely due to his race, President Obama's White House finally stepped in—not to defend a fellow liberal administrator, but to praise the rabblerousing students. White House press secretary Josh Earnest said that this was the sort of activity Obama talked about "in his campaign, that a few people speaking up and speaking out can have a profound impact on the communities where we live and work."

Community organizing on a national scale. President Obama's vision has finally reached fruition. And because the tree of leftism must occasionally be watered with the blood of liberal authority figures, Tim Wolfe is out of a job. But no big deal. Such are the wages of "white privilege."

No, It Is Not Un-American to Prefer Christian Refugees to Muslim Refugees

November 18, 2015

On Friday, Muslim terrorists murdered 129 people in Paris. At least one of the ISIS perpetrators apparently entered Europe as a "refugee" from Syria—he was found with a refugee ID. ISIS has already claimed that they have infiltrated the Syrian refugee population to the tune of thousands of terrorists.

On Monday, President Obama announced that it would be purely un-American for Westerners to ban unvetted Muslim immigrants from the Middle East while allowing Christian targets of genocide to enter the West. He called such an idea "shameful," while passionately calling for Americans to "open our hearts" to more refugees. He praised bordering countries Turkey, Jordan and Lebanon for taking in hundreds of thousands of refugees; Obama said that showed their "belief in a common humanity." He added, "And so we have to, each of us, do our part. And the United States has to step up and do its part. And when I hear folks say that, well, maybe we should just admit the Christians but not the Muslims ...That's not American. That's not who we are."

Every aspect of this little speech is wrong. Turkey, Jordan and Lebanon aren't taking in Muslim refugees out of some great commitment to common humanity. They're doing so because their other choice involves setting up fences and machine guns to stop the waves of refugees crossing their frontiers. And as we know, Muslim countries have a rotten history of absorbing fellow members of their ummah: For 70 years, since the creation of the State of Israel, tens of thousands of Palestinian Arabs have lived in refugee camps located in Muslim lands. By contrast, the State of Israel has taken in every

Jewish refugee seeking asylum, from Russian emigres to Moroccan immigrants, from Ethiopian refugees to Syrian expatriates.

And the West has good reason for skepticism toward Muslim refugees. While Muslim refugees who stay in the Middle East split evenly between males and females, the vast majority of refugees entering Europe are males of fighting age. Muslim immigration has already led to massive increases in crime from France to Sweden, and cultural fragmentation from Great Britain to Austria. Terrorism is only the latest threat—and even that threat is obviously not exaggerated. Vetting refugees from Syria is nearly impossible given its status as a failed state. Vetting Muslim refugees is totally impossible given the fact that radical Muslims can easily masquerade as less-radical Muslims.

So why does President Obama, along with the global left, seek more Muslim immigration? Because President Obama does not believe that Islam, as a religious philosophy, presents any threat to the West. He believes that radical Islam doesn't exist. It's merely the hallmark of global poverty, probably affected negatively by climate change; if the West redistributed its wealth, ceased its "colonial" attitudes toward the Middle East, all would be well. The materialism of Marxism would win the day.

Never mind that this argument is entirely without evidence. Never mind that Muslims from Western nations have left wealth to join the impoverished ISIS fighters. Never mind that Osama Bin Laden himself was a wealthy man who lived in a cave to plan attacks against Westerners. Ideology matters, but to the self-centered Marxists of the global left, only their ideology matters: Everyone else has merely fallen into nasty ideas thanks to lack of resources.

And so we must give them our resources, endanger our own citizens. To do anything else would be un-American, according to the people whose idea of Americanism involves the rejection of the very ideas upon which America was founded.

The Death of Free Speech

November 25, 2015

Four in 10 young Americans have no idea what America is.

That's the takeaway from a new Pew Research poll showing that 40 percent of Americans aged 18-34 say that the government should be able to prevent people from making "statements that are offensive to minority groups." This same group of young people has granted broad awareness to the culture of "microaggression"—unintended slights taken as grave insults by their victims; they've also called for "trigger warnings," alerts that certain communications may dredge up unpleasant past memories or ideas. With such ghoulish cruelties haunting the most privileged generation in human history, naturally we'd want to toss out the bedrock of Western civilization: The right to debate, to express unpopular opinions. We wouldn't want to offend.

Unless, of course, we do.

There are those of us who find guns in our face far more offensive than the occasional taunt. We don't like the notion that your disapproval of an opinion gives you the right to call the men with the guns; we find that perspective tyrannical and threatening. We're not interested in your subjective feelings-world, in which you claim that innocuous statements somehow harm you in material ways. We don't believe that self-appointed victim status grants you the ability to use force. We think you ought to develop a thicker skin—the sort of skin necessary to enjoy freedom. If your political agoraphobia prevents you from engaging in the arguments that characterize free countries, that doesn't mean you should lock us all away in our "safe spaces." Those "safe spaces" are called jail cells, and the only people who want to establish them are jackbooted fascists masquerading as hippy-dippy caring experts.

If all of this seems relatively basic, that's because it is. But because America forgot to teach her children those basics, they will be torn out by the root. The American university system has become Ground Zero for the anti-free speech movement. That's because young people always look for a cause for which to fight, an oppressive force to crush. Young people aren't looking for comfort; as George Orwell wrote in 1940 regarding the appeal of the Nazis, "Nearly all western thought since the last war, certainly all 'progressive' thought, has assumed tacitly that human beings desire nothing beyond ease, security and avoidance of pain. In such a view of life there is no room, for instance, for patriotism and the military virtues. Hitler, because in his own joyless mind he feels it with exceptional strength, knows that human beings don't only want comfort, safety, short working-hours, hygiene, birth-control and, in general, common sense; they also, at least intermittently, want struggle and self-sacrifice, not to mention drums, flags and loyalty-parades."

How can today's young people enjoy such struggle?

Since America is the freest country in the history of humanity, the only oppression to be found is self-oppression—and the only way to free people from that is to shackle everyone else. The old rule of politics stated that your right to wave your fist ends with my nose; the leftist perspective is that your right to wave your fist ends with that waving fist generating feelings of unease. So stop waving it. Anywhere.

The real danger here is that the would-be oppressors will win. They already are on university campuses, where those labeled holders of "white privilege" can now be fired or silenced based on the color of their skin. If Americans don't fight back against the free speech opponents, this battle will get ugly: Once one side utilizes actual aggression, it's only a matter of time until battle truly begins.

President Obama's Imaginary World

December 2, 2015

President Obama lives in a world all his own. It's a world in which he's widely beloved but also misunderstood, a world in which everyone is racist except for those who support him, a world in which his foreign policy has been heroically successful and his domestic policy even more so. President Obama lives in Fantasyland.

In this Fantasyland, it's not enough for President Obama to define the world around him in self-serving fashion. He must define his enemies the same way. To that end, while visiting Paris for the Climate Change Summit that will supposedly usher in an era of global cooperation and environmental utopianism, Obama announced that he had finally found a way to defeat Islamic State. Talking about climate change, Obama said, was an "act of defiance that proves nothing will deter us ... What greater rejection of those who would tear down our world than marshaling our best efforts to save it?"

Not to be Debbie Downer, but nothing in ISIS' plans suggests that they care deeply about preventing a bunch of self-important bureaucrats from meeting in well-stocked, toney hotels to destroy the Western economy on behalf of scientific chimeras. ISIS, in fact, probably adores the notion that the West will take itself down a couple economic pegs in order to redistribute the wealth. Certainly other Islamic terrorists have felt that way. Osama Bin Laden, for example, lamented that the West did not spend more money on climate change relief efforts, and stated according to Al Jazeera, "Speaking about climate change is not a matter of intellectual luxury—the phenomenon is an actual fact. All of the industrialized countries, especially the big ones, bear responsibility for the global warming crisis."

Regardless of ISIS' feelings on global warming, they obviously don't sit around in Raqqa lamenting that their plans have been defeated by those dastardly Westerners and their catered diplomatic lunches. But President Obama says they do. That's because he crafts his own enemies based on who he wishes they were. Obama is thoroughly uncomfortable with the idea that those who wish to fight him are members of radical Islam. He wishes they were right-wing American ideologues. So he simply plays them off as such.

Obama did the same thing with regard to the Iran nuclear deal. While handing Iran $150 billion in funding, opening their economy, and granting them a full nuclear weapons program in a decade, Obama claimed that the real enemies of peace were Republicans siding with Iranian hardliners. Never mind that those hardliners didn't exist. Obama created them magically, and then made them Republicans.

Barack Obama is a leftist hammer in search of a conservative nail. No matter who his enemies *actually* are, he'll characterize them as American conservatives for purposes of whacking them over the head. ISIS may have slaughtered Westerners in Paris thanks to radical Islam, but Obama will never acknowledge that: instead, he'll just claim that they're essentially Ted Cruz in keffiyehs.

This isn't rare. Jackie Kennedy once lamented that her husband had been shot by a "silly little communist" rather than dying for civil rights; her allies quickly turned JFK's assassination into a referendum on American conservatism. Obama's doing the same thing now. He has chosen his enemies, and they don't include ISIS. That means that if ISIS must be his enemy, he will simply wave his Fantasyland wand, and they will be transformed into the Republican enemies he so craves.

The problem is, they won't. They'll just keep killing. Reality remains reality, no matter how much President Obama sprinkles fairy dust and claps his hands.

Should We Religiously Profile?

December 9, 2015

Months ago, a concerned American at a school in Texas spotted a 14-year-old Muslim boy toting around a contraption that looked very much like a bomb. That Texan called the police, who came and detained the boy; after learning that the boy's device was actually a disassembled clock, they released him.

Weeks ago, a concerned American in San Bernardino spotted a "half-dozen Middle Eastern men" in the area of an apartment housing Syed Rizwan Farook and Tashfeen Malik. He didn't know what they were doing there, but they seemed suspicious. He didn't call the cops.

In San Bernardino, of course, that political correctness ended in the death of 14 Americans and the wounding of 21 more. In Texas, that failure to bow to political correctness ended in the attorney general of the United States vowing to track down and investigate the local police department.

Welcome to politically correct America, where you are damned if you do, and damned if you don't.

Political correctness costs lives. It doesn't merely require us to abide by the strictures of an arbitrary linguistic code. It isn't just an irritation. It means that we're all supposed to frontally lobotomize ourselves to basic realities. We're supposed to pretend that there's nothing more suspicious about a half-dozen Middle Eastern males coming and going at odd hours from an apartment with a small child than there would be if a half-dozen white males did the same thing. We're supposed to cave to the fantasy that a religious Muslim reaching out to terrorists over the internet poses no more threat than a Christian visiting a pro-life website. We're supposed to blind ourselves in order to avoid the obvious.

That costs lives.

Now, this doesn't mean that we ought to discriminate against individual Muslims, of course. But it does mean that law enforcement ought to look at indicators of possible terrorist connections, and that one preliminary indicator is religious practice of Islam. That indicator isn't sufficient to determine connection to terrorism—far from it. No single indicator generally is. But behavioral profiling involves investigating a variety of factors. As Daniel Wagner, CEO of Risk Solutions, writes about Israel's profiling techniques, "Departing passengers [at Ben Gurion Airport] are questioned by highly trained security agents before they reach the check-in counter. These interviews could last as little as one minute or as long as an hour, based on such factors as age, race, religion and destination."

Ignoring any of these factors represents incompetence.

But the president wants to use the force of law to enshrine incompetence. He suggests that to assess risk differently based on religious observance is somehow a violation of basic American principles, rather than a time-tested technique of all human relations. We obviously must remain on guard for baseless bias and persecution without evidence. But we can't ignore the realities of risk assessment in the name of cultural sensitivity, either.

That's how we end up with the utter stupidity of an MSNBC host suggesting that media stop showing pictures of the San Bernardino female shooter so as not to link her hijab-clad visage with Islam. That's how we end up with Obama suggesting that our own Islamophobia causes terrorism, rather than radical Islam. Most importantly, that's how we end up with more dead Americans.

Security Dies Where Multiculturalism Thrives

December 16, 2015

While Americans fret over Donald Trump's plans to ban Muslim immigration to the United States temporarily thanks to the government's inability to keep us safe, the government continues to prove its inability to keep us safe. This week, we found out that President Obama's Department of Homeland Security prohibited agents from screening foreign citizens applying for visas to enter the country. According to former acting undersecretary at DHS for intelligence and analysis John Cohen, "During that time period immigration officials were not allowed to use or review social media as part of the screening process. ... The primary concern was that it would be viewed negatively if it was disclosed publicly and there were concerns that it would be embarrassing."

He continued, "It was primarily a question of optics. There were concerns from a privacy and civil liberties perspective that while this was not illegal, that it would be viewed negatively if it was disclosed publicly."

So 14 Americans in San Bernardino died for optics.

While President Obama insists that the government must check the metadata of American citizens to catch terrorists, he insists that his own people stop checking the publicly posted Facebook messages of potential terrorists.

This is the essence of multiculturalism. Multiculturalism suggests that all cultures are equal, that they carry equal values, that they pose equal threats to public safety. Extending that logic, we must treat suspects from all cultures with equal care. But what if not all cultures provide an equal threat? What if the people who engage in some cultures are more likely than others to participate in terrorism? Then, in order to maintain the multicultural fiction, we must bend over backwards not to check out threats from such cultures. Either that, or we must violate everyone's civil rights equally.

The former is happening in the United States; the latter is happening in France, where the government has been knocking down the doors of hundreds of mosques on grounds of "preach[ing] hatred" or using "takfiri speech," according to French imam Hassan El Alaoui. In the United States, we'd see such raids as a violation of the First and Fourth Amendments. In France, they have no such amendments. They do, however, have a multicultural view of the world.

Or at least they did. Across Europe, the reality of multiculturalism is hitting home. German chancellor Angela Merkel, who was recently named Time's Person of the Year for taking in one million Syrian refugees, said, "Multiculturalism leads to parallel societies and therefore remains a 'life lie' ... We want and we will reduce the number of refugees noticeably." She was forced to denounce her own former viewpoint thanks to the fallout from her decisions: Refugee camps have turned into hotbeds of rape and child abuse. Mass Muslim immigration into Europe has heightened such challenges for years, of course, but the left and the press have suppressed such information.

No longer.

This is what happens when the West denies its values. Eventually, reality forces the West to confront the truth: Its own culture is superior to others, and that pretending otherwise creates real danger. But so long as leftists like President Obama remain in denial, that danger will only grow.

Hillary Is the Islamic State's Best Recruitment Tool

December 23, 2015

During the little-watched pre-Christmas Democratic debate, former Secretary of State Hillary Clinton accused Donald Trump of being the Islamic State group's chief recruiter. Relying on her penchant for blaming videos for Islamic evil, she stated that the Islamic State is "showing videos of Donald Trump insulting Islam and Muslims in order to recruit more radical jihadists."

Well, no.

The Islamic State's videos—the ones that actually exist, not the ones Clinton makes up in her fevered imagination during debate pee breaks—show that the group uses three main themes in its recruitment. First, it talks about Islamic prophecy. In a video released Nov. 24, titled "No Respite," the narrator explains, in English, over hypnotic chanting: "This is our (caliphate), in all its glory, remaining and expanding. ... It's a state built on the prophetic methodology, striving to follow the Quran and Sunna. ... We are men honored with Islam who climbed its peaks to perform jihad, answering the call to unite under one flag. This is the source of our glory: our obedience to our Lord. ... We only bow to Allah."

So much for President Barack Obama and Hillary Clinton's jabbering nonsensically about the Islamic State's having nothing to do with Islam.

Second, it talks about its string of victories. The video brags that the group's territory is "already greater than Britain, eight times the size of Belgium and 30 times the size of Qatar." It directly challenges America: "You claim to have the greatest army history has known. You may have the numbers and weapons, but your soldiers lack the will and resolve. Still scarred from their defeats in Afghanistan and Iraq, they return dead or suicidal, with over 6,500 of them killing themselves each year." It claims that America's airstrikes have accomplished nothing and that the United States' $250,000 missiles will never be able to defeat the Islamic State and its 50-cent bullets. It adds that the United States lacks the power to put boots on the ground.

In other words, it mocks the Obama administration's agenda. Without losses in Afghanistan and Iraq—both idiotic and precipitous pullouts by the Obama team—and without the constant drumbeat from the left that military men and women are poor victims of circumstance, the Islamic State wouldn't have this particular talking point.

Finally, the Islamic State talks about the emptiness of the West. The group contrasts its own allegiance to Allah with the West's allegiance to "a secular state—built on man-made laws—whose soldiers fight for the interests of ... legislators, liars, fornicators, corporations and for the freedoms of sodomites." The video flashes pictures of Obama, George W. Bush and Bill Clinton. No Trump.

It concludes: "Bring it on, all of you. Your numbers only increase us in faith, and we're counting your banners, which our prophet said would reach 80 in number, and then the flames of war will finally burn you on the hills of Dabiq. Bring it on, for we echo the mighty call of our prophets. ... Show us no respite. Our ally is the greatest. He is Allah, and all glory belongs to him." The reference to Dabiq is to an apocalyptic site in Syria. According to Islamic teachings, it is supposed to host a battle between the Christians and the Muslims that will usher in Armageddon.

So as it turns out, it isn't Trump whom the Islamic State uses to recruit. It's the American government—in particular the victories handed to the group by the American left. Hillary Clinton is a better recruiting tool for the Islamic State than Donald Trump, hands down.

For Obama, It's Not Delusion, It's Purpose

December 30, 2015

Good news, America: the Obama administration has achieved peace in Syria. That's according to John Kirby, the Assistant Secretary of State for the Bureau of Public Affairs and spokesperson at the US State Department, who issued a blog post filled with five-word summations of 2015. Here's their summation of the Syrian crisis: "Bringing Peace, Security to Syria."

So the hundreds of thousands dead, the millions of refugees, the rise of ISIS, the enshrinement of dictator Bashar Assad—none of it ever happened. According to the State Department, everything's going swimmingly.

More good news: the Obama administration has also defeated terrorism: "Winning Fight Against Violent Extremists." Oddly, more Americans now say that America is losing the war on terrorism than at any time since 9/11; 74 percent of Americans say they are dissatisfied with how the war on terror is progressing.

But the news gets even better: the State Department proclaims that it has achieved Iran's disarmament: "Iran Peaceful Nuclear Program Ensured." Well, there is that whole awkward Iran continuing to develop whatever it wants while funding terrorism across the world with money freed up by the United States and its allies. But really, we've stopped the mullahs dead in their tracks.

There are only two possible rationales for this sort of disconnect with reality: first, the Obama administration knows they're full of it, but they keep on gritting their teeth and pushing the misinformation; second, they seriously believe that they are achieving magnificent results. In other words, they're either cynical or delusional.

My money's on delusional.

Barack Obama is a pseudo-intellectual who believes so deeply in the power of his own ideas that he gets lost in them. It never occurs to him that they could breed violence or evil. They're beautiful. Like Dr. Manhattan in "Watchmen," he'd rather build crystal towers of stunning meticulousness on Mars than anything of value here on Earth—but unlike Dr. Manhattan, he won't leave Earth alone. He'll transplant his notions of reality onto the rest of us.

Thus alleged deserter Bowe Bergdahl becomes a soldier who served honorably; Benghazi becomes a battle over a YouTube video; Israel becomes the aggressor against the peaceful Palestinians; ISIS becomes a jayvee threat; Iran becomes a potential ally. Obama has done the calculations on his chalkboard, and they all add up.

Except that they don't. But that won't stop Obama from pursuing his equations, thinking himself the John Nash who revolutionized game theory when he's actually the John Nash pasting headlines about the communist conspiracy to the walls of his study. It's all still beautiful in his head. It's just delusional.

And that delusion has real world costs. This week, we found out that Obama pressured Secretary of Defense Ash Carter to release more Guantanamo Bay terrorists into foreign hands, and even scolded him personally. Reuters reports, "Since then, the Pentagon has been more cooperative. Administration officials said they expect to begin transferring at least 17 detainees to foreign countries in January." The report said Obama fired Carter's predecessor, Chuck Hagel, for slow-walking Gitmo transfers as well.

That's because the Defense Department still has to operate in the realm of reality, where nearly 30 percent of Gitmo releases have either been confirmed re-entering the fray or are suspected of having done so. Obama doesn't have to worry about such realities. He's busy constructing crystal castles on Mars.

Except Mars is right here, on Earth.

And Obama's still the most powerful man on this planet.

~~~

About the Author

Ben Shapiro was born in 1984. He entered the University of California Los Angeles at the age of 16 and graduated summa cum laude and Phi Beta Kappa in June 2004 with a Bachelor of Arts degree in Political Science. He graduated Harvard Law School cum laude in June 2007.

Shapiro was hired by Creators Syndicate at age 17 to become the youngest nationally syndicated columnist in the United States. His columns are printed in major newspapers and websites including *The Riverside Press-Enterprise* and the *Conservative Chronicle*, Townhall.com, ABCNews.com, WorldNetDaily.com, Human Events, FrontPageMag.com, FamilySecurityMatters.com. His columns have appeared in *The Christian Science Monitor, Chicago Sun-Times, Orlando Sentinel, The Honolulu Advertiser, The Arizona Republic, Claremont Review of Books* and RealClearPolitics.com. He has been the subject of articles by *The Wall Street Journal, The New York Times*, The Associated Press, and *The Christian Science Monitor*; he has been quoted on "The Rush Limbaugh Show," "The Dr. Laura Show," at CBSNews.com, in the *New York Press, The Washington Times*, and *The American Conservative*.

The author of the national best-sellers, "Brainwashed: How Universities Indoctrinate America's Youth," "Porn Generation: How Social Liberalism Is Corrupting Our Future," and "Project President:

Bad Hair and Botox on the Road to the White House." Shapiro has appeared on hundreds of television and radio shows around the nation, including "The O'Reilly Factor," "Fox and Friends," "In the Money," "DaySide with Linda Vester," "Scarborough Country," "The Dennis Miller Show," "Fox News Live," "Glenn Beck Show," "Your World with Neil Cavuto," "700 Club," "The Laura Ingraham Show," "The Michael Medved Show," "The G. Gordon Liddy Show," "The Rusty Humphries Show," "The Lars Larson Show," "The Larry Elder Show," The Hugh Hewitt Show" and "The Dennis Prager Show."

Shapiro is married and runs Benjamin Shapiro Legal Consulting in Los Angeles.

~~~

EVIL IN AMERICA
is also available as an e-book
for Kindle, Amazon Fire, iPad, Nook and
Android e-readers. Visit
creatorspublishing.com to learn more.

o o o

CREATORS PUBLISHING

We publish books.
We find compelling storytellers and
help them craft their narrative,
distributing their novels and collections
worldwide.

o o o

48630969R00073

Made in the USA
Middletown, DE
23 September 2017